little italy

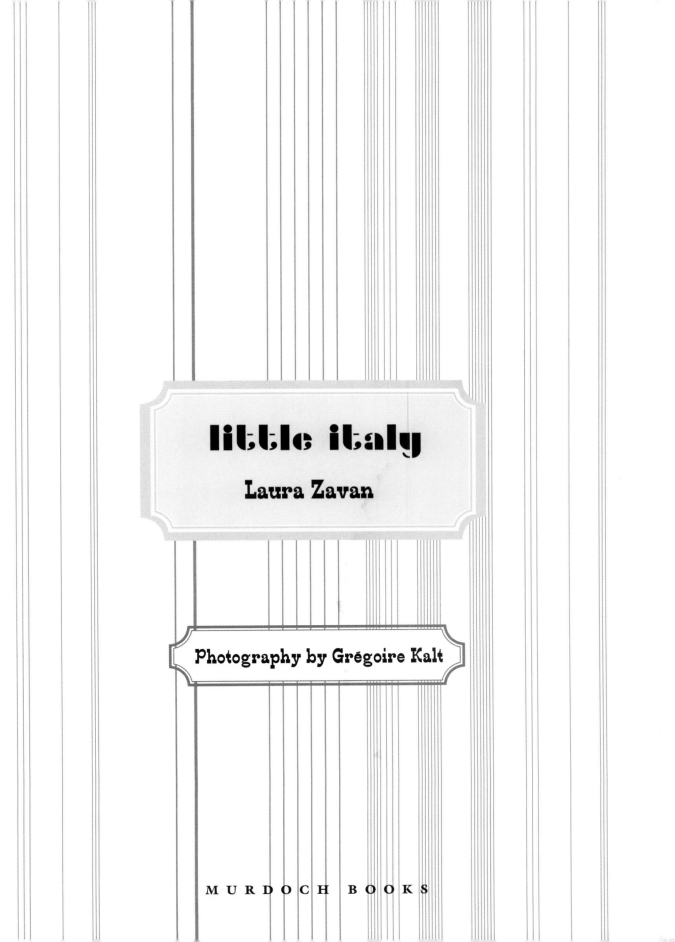

little italy

Laura Zavan

Photography by Grégoire Kalt

MURDOCH BOOKS

FOREWORD

This book has come from a desire to share my enthusiasm and passion for the Italian products which are a everyday gourmet pleasure for me...

No matter where I find myself, I always seek out my own Italy: salted capers, ventresca tuna, fresh mozzarella and burrata cheeses, amaretti biscuits and so on. I love products with flavours simple enough to make a great dish that's not too elaborate: for me, this is what Italian cooking is... burrata cheese spread on a pizza bianca, a drizzle of olive oil, a turn of the pepper mill. Troppo buono! No more is needed for a feast.

I have used these typical ingredients as a starting point to provide you with ideas and recipes (some personal favourites but also classics). I think this results in a form of cooking that's accessible to everyone, simple, quick and natural. Track down a good Italian grocery store and always have a small stock of survival rations on hand for every occasion.

I have my own 'Ali Baba's cave' at home, a little overwhelming sometimes (a hazard of my profession and family I tell myself...), but thanks to which I am always able to prepare wonderful meals under any circumstances and survive crisis situations in regal fashion (such as writing a book and not leaving the house for several weeks!).

Buon appetito!

Laura

antipasti

Olives

I prefer to buy olives loose and often ask to taste them. Whether black or green, there is an incredible number of varieties, but my favourites are the little taggiasca olives from Liguria; black, pitted olives, sweet and tasty, which I use for all of my recipes … Try them out and you'll be hooked! In some delicatessens you can find olive ascolane, large green olives stuffed with meat then crumbed and fried. These olives must be tried at least once in a lifetime …

Olive paste

Ready-made versions are widely available. Read the labels carefully and buy the ones that are made only from olives, extra-virgin olive oil and herbs.

Serve with drinks, spread on bread, crostini or lingue crispbreads. Top with halved cherry tomatoes and small basil leaves. It makes a change from the ubiquitous tapenade.

Use to flavour a pasta salad with vegetables (tomatoes, capsicum and grilled eggplant).Use to season a beef, tuna or swordfish carpaccio, to which you can add a few leaves of rocket and some cherry tomatoes.

With drinks

Offer a few different kinds of olive. Combine them or serve separately in small bowls.

In a salad

The milder varieties go very well with a tomato, mozzarella and basil salad.

In a sauce

Add a few anchovy fillets, finely chopped olives, rinsed salted capers, oregano or basil to a tomato sauce (for pasta or pizza).

In cooking

To flavour fish (mullet, bream, bass, tuna or swordfish) and meats (chicken or rabbit), add a few crushed olives during cooking.

Home-made olive paste

Combine in a processor (or chop by hand), 200 g pitted olives (black or green) with 1 or 2 tablespoons of dried herbs (oregano, marjoram, rosemary or thyme) or with the equivalent of a bunch of fresh herbs (basil, parsley, chives). Lightly season and add olive oil in a stream until a paste. (For 4 people.)

Use it with ...?

Olive paste and ricotta for crostini, or enjoy with slices of prosciutto. For a marbled effect, carefully mix 2 tablespoons of black olive paste or some finely chopped black olives with 250 g ricotta.

Olive, caper and anchovy paste for crostini and pasta. Process black olive paste with 50 g rinsed salted capers, 6–8 anchovy fillets and 1 clove crushed garlic.

Olive paste with chilli for pasta. Add dried or fresh chilli to your home-made olive paste with plenty of chopped parsley.

Storage ...

Keep loose olives and olive paste in the refrigerator, covered with olive oil. Use within two weeks.

Pomodori sott'olio

Sun-dried tomatoes

These are available whole or as a paste. They must be preserved in olive oil, be neither too salty nor too vinegary, and above all remain tender! The best ones come from the tip of Sicily (Pachino), which has an exceptional climate and yields sun-soaked fruit.

With drinks

Serve them plain on a slice of bread. It's the best way to enjoy them! To impress your guests, make up mini-kebabs of sun-dried tomato and provola cheese (smoked mozzarella), instead of a buffalo mozzarella (whose taste will be masked by the tomato).

In a salad

Or in a panino, with canned tuna in oil, olives, basil and rinsed salted capers, or some provola cheese.

In a sauce

In a food processor, roughly combine 8 sun-dried tomatoes and 100 g blanched almonds. Mix in 500 g diced fresh tomatoes, and 1 crushed garlic clove, olive oil, salt and freshly ground black pepper.

Home-made sun-dried tomato paste

Process 200 g marinated sun-dried tomatoes, 2 tablespoons of dried herbs (oregano, thyme, rosemary, marjoram) or 2 bunches of basil and 1 garlic clove. Season very lightly and add olive oil in a stream until the desired consistency is obtained. (For 4 people.)

Spread on crostini and top with half an olive and basil. If you prefer a creamier taste, add a little ricotta and mix lightly for a marbled effect.

To flavour a pasta salad, supplement the paste with chopped olives, oregano, basil or chopped rocket and finally, a good canned tuna in oil or some anchovies.

For a pesto, add 50 g grated Pecorino Romano or parmesan cheese. Or try it with a nice, hard sheep's milk cheese, it's delicious.

Home-made preserves

Buy a packet of sun-dried tomatoes (without oil) and immerse them for a few minutes in lightly vinegared, boiling water. Drain them thoroughly on paper towels. Put in sterilised, airtight jars, cover with olive oil and add unpeeled garlic cloves, herbs (oregano, rosemary, thyme), capers and chilli. Wait 3 weeks before eating so they become imbued with all of the flavours. Use the oil to enhance salads or pasta.

Home-made semi-dried tomatoes

Sweeter and more delicate than sun-dried tomatoes, these are an ideal accompaniment to meat or fish.

Make an incision in some tomatoes (I prefer the roma variety), plunge them in boiling water for a few seconds then run them under cold water. Remove the skin, quarter them lengthways, remove the seeds. Arrange them in a single layer on a baking tray with a drizzle of olive oil, some crushed garlic cloves, oregano, thyme, salt and freshly ground black pepper. Cook them in the oven at 90°C for 2 hours. Keep them in the refrigerator in an airtight container, and use within a short period of time.

Peperoni Capsicum

Marinated grilled capsicums can be used in a thousand ways. You will find them ready-made at delicatessen counters. They must be marinated in plenty of oil but avoid marinades that contain vinegar: it masks the taste of the capsicum.

Home-made grilled capsicums

Cut capsicums in two, remove the seeds and put them, skin side up, on a baking tray lined with baking paper and grill (broil) on high. Check them frequently. As soon as they blister, but before they burn, put them in a bowl, cover with plastic wrap and allow them to cool. Remove the skin and marinate for a few hours with some olive oil, crushed garlic, basil (or other herbs), salt and freshly ground black pepper.

As a starter

Combine marinated, grilled capsicums with olives, capers, anchovies, rocket and enjoy with olive oil grissini, focaccia or in a salad.

In pasta or on a pizza

Slice the capsicums into thin strips or finely dice. Combined with lots of basil, grated ricotta salata or diced mozzarella, it's magnificent!

As an accompaniment

Try with poultry or grilled lamb. They are also perfect with tuna or swordfish.

Stuffed capsicums

With tuna. Process 300 g well-drained canned tuna in oil with 1 tablespoon of salted capers (preferably rinsed), 2 tablespoons of pitted black olives, 1 teaspoon of oregano, 2 anchovy fillets, olive oil, and a little salt and pepper. Spread this mixture on 8 grilled capsicum halves, roll up and serve with dressed rocket. (For 4 people.)

Combine with cheese and mint. Process 150 g ricotta cheese (preferably sheep's milk ricotta) with 150 g fresh goat's cheese, a handful of mint leaves, olive oil, salt and freshly ground black pepper until a paste. Spread this mixture on 8 grilled capsicum halves, roll up and serve with a mesclun salad. (For 4 people.)

Tip

To keep grilled capsicums for several months, put them in an airtight jar and cover with olive oil. Once the jar is opened, consume within a short period of time.

Carciofi SOTT'OLIO Marinated artichokes

Italians are mad for this vegetable. The Roman ones are used for preserving as they are small, tender and have almost no 'choke' inside. You will find jars of them in almost every food store or sold by weight at the delicatessen counter. Check that they are swimming in olive oil and ensure they are tender and have a low vinegar content. You can also find jars of plain artichoke paste, along with varieties containing almonds, anchovies, etc.

With drinks

Choose small artichoke hearts and serve them with bread, grissini or lingue crispbread. Offer toothpicks to avoid oil all over people's fingers.

In a panino or salad

Add artichokes to a panino or salad along with bresaola (dried beef) or Prosciutto di Parma and some rocket.

Crostini

I also like to serve crostini spread with artichoke paste and garnished with parsley and toasted almonds or pine nuts.

Home-made preserves

You will need 1 kg small Roman artichokes, 1 litre white vinegar (6 percent acidity), 1 litre water, 1 lemon, 30 g coarse salt, 2 bay leaves, 1 teaspoon of cloves, 1 tablespoon of peppercorns and olive oil.

Clean the artichokes (discard the toughest outer leaves) and immerse immediately in water with lemon juice added so they don't discolour.

Plunge them into the boiling salted and vinegared water. Allow 8 to 10 minutes cooking time once they return to the boil (if you cut them into two or four pieces, then halve the cooking time). Drain well and allow them to dry on a clean tea towel for at least 1 hour.

Put the artichoke hearts in completely dry preserving jars, alternating with the herbs and spices, and cover with olive oil. Add some more oil the next day if needed. Wait for one month before eating.

If you want to keep them for longer, sterilise the jars. Wash jars in soapy water, rinse again. Boil in a large pot of water for 10 minutes, drain upside down on a clean cloth. Dry completely in a 150°C oven. Remove and fill jars whilst still hot. (20 minutes for 250 g, 30 minutes for 500 g or 40 minutes for 750 g).

Home-made artichoke paste

Process 200 g preserved artichoke hearts (well-drained) with fresh or dried herbs (for example, parsley, mint or thyme), 100 g toasted and chopped blanched almonds, or 6 canned anchovy fillets in oil. Season with salt and pepper to your liking.

Assortment of antipasti (from Delitaly)

Acciughe Anchovies

This little fish is ultra-rich in omega-3s and easy to use in cooking. Mediterranean anchovies are sold preserved (in oil or brine) and as a paste (in tubes or jars).

Anchovies in olive oil

Don't skimp on quality. For an impromptu snack with drinks, generously butter a few slices of crusty bread and top with a well-drained anchovy and a pinch of oregano.

Crostini with mascarpone-anchovy cream

Chop 100 g anchovies in oil (or use anchovy paste) and mix with 250 g mascarpone cheese, 1 handful of rinsed salted capers and 2 teaspoons of oregano. (For 4 people.)

Panino

Try out a combination of anchovies, hard-boiled eggs and capers; anchovies and grilled capsicum; or anchovies, tomatoes, capers and olives. Try as well a few anchovies with canned tuna.

Anchovies in brine

These are sold by weight in some fishmongers, or in jars and vacuum-packed in gourmet food stores and delicatessens. Rinse under running water, remove the backbone and separate the fillets. They are ideal for flavouring tomato, capsicum and eggplant-based sauces. They also add character to many fish or meat dishes.

Spaghetti with anchovies

A recipe typical of the area around Venice. Soften 3 chopped bulb spring onions and 8 brined anchovy fillets in 100 ml olive oil over low heat. Moisten with a little water as needed so that the sauce doesn't stick. You should have quite a thick paste. Mix into spaghetti cooked until al dente.

Breadcrumbs with anchovies

Scatter anchovy breadcrumbs over pasta with tomato sauce, fish or vegetables as a change from parmesan cheese. Gently heat 2 tablespoons of olive oil in a frying pan to sauté 2 quartered garlic cloves and 4 finely chopped brined anchovy fillets. When the anchovies have completely disintegrated, add 4 heaped tablespoons of crumbled stale bread or breadcrumbs. Combine well over the heat so that the breadcrumbs are golden. (For 4 people.)

Bagna cauda

This Piedmontese recipe is perfect for an informal dinner. Following the same principle as a fondue, place the sauce in the middle of the table, on a dish-warmer. Dip your own choice of raw or cooked vegetables (cauliflower, capsicum, Jerusalem artichoke, purple artichoke, potato) and fried cubes of polenta. I also like to use this recipe as a base for stuffing tomatoes.

At least 1 hour ahead of time, soak 3 garlic cloves in 100 ml milk (this will make the garlic more digestible), then drain and crush. In a small earthenware casserole dish (or a saucepan), melt 60 g butter over a very low heat, then add 200 ml olive oil, the crushed garlic and 150 g rinsed anchovy fillets.

TONNO Tuna

Every part of the tuna is good. In Sicily and Sardinia, the fish are brought close to the coast with a net and then caught with a harpoon. The tuna bleed out completely into the sea so their flesh is therefore better suited for canning and preserves than tuna that are line-caught on the open sea. The tastiest is the Mediterranean bluefin tuna, the guilty indulgence of connoisseurs. As a matter of course, it is also the most expensive. However, you can use the delicately flavoured white albacore tuna as a substitute. Avoid the yellowfin tuna caught in the Atlantic as its flesh tends to be quite bland.

Tips for buying

Choose fish that is marinated in olive oil and sold in glass jars so you have a better idea of the colour and size of the pieces. Drain before using. Once opened, cover with oil for storing and use within a week.

The best pieces are taken from the loin. The ultimate is ventresca tuna (premium belly meat), which is fatty and tender. Another choice part for tuna lovers is the tarantello (from the belly closer to the back), which is leaner and has a fine flavour. You can also find canned or preserved tuna sold under the name 'buzzonaglia': the pieces are taken from the humbler parts of the fish but are very tender and have a pleasant flavour (they can be used to make delicious recipes). At least once, buy the 'lattume', the reproductive organs of the fish marinated in oil, which can be sliced and served with oil, lemon and fresh parsley.

Ideas

Use in a salad with potatoes, thin slices of bulb spring onion, parsley and olive oil, or with dried beans (borlotti or white beans) and onions.

Ultra-simple: panini or crostini topped with tuna in oil.

Make a typically Italian salad by combining bluefin tuna with fresh or sun-dried tomatoes, black olives, rinsed salted capers, a little oregano and a drizzle of olive oil. As a variation, add a few grilled capsicums. Take the same ingredients and mix them into pasta or rice for a more substantial dish. You can also chop it finely and use it to stuff tomatoes or capsicum.

For smaller budgets

Good canned and preserved tuna is quite expensive. As a substitute, buy mackerel fillets in olive oil. They're delicious in a salad with a few tomatoes. The best products are canned in Sicily.

bottarga Caviar of the Mediterranean Sea

Grey mullet or tuna roe are washed, salted, pressed and dried. They are eaten in thin slices or grated over pasta or eggs. Grey mullet bottarga has a lovely amber colour and a delicate flavour. It is sold vacuum-packed or covered with beeswax or paraffin. The most renowned bottarga comes from Sardinia. Tuna bottarga has a more salty taste and melting texture. You can also find grated bottarga, very practical for sprinkling over pasta and above all it is quite economical, but it is not as tasty as real bottarga. Once opened, bottarga keeps for a week wrapped in plastic wrap.

On crostini, lingue ...

Coarsely grate onto buttered bread, serve bottarga shavings dressed with olive oil or truffle-flavoured oil, or make a pesto for spreading by mixing grated bottarga, crushed pistachio nuts and a drizzle of olive oil.

In a salad

Serve bottarga shavings with cherry tomatoes, celery or white beans. Add a drizzle of olive oil, salt and freshly ground black pepper to season the whole mix.

Shaved or grated

Serve bottarga on pasta cooked al dente, with a large knob of butter and chopped parsley. Following the same principle, use this combination with white rice. Also try pasta with a pesto of pistachio and bottarga, tuna bottarga shavings on fried or scrambled eggs or thin escalopes of veal, floured and pan-fried in butter.

Bottarga butter

Mix 80 g softened butter with 20 g grated bottarga. Roll up into a sausage shape in baking paper and refrigerate until firm. Spread on crostini or use slices to flavour grilled white meats.

Spaghetti with an oil, garlic, chilli and bottarga sauce

On a very low heat, sauté 2 garlic cloves in 4 tablespoons of olive oil. Remove the garlic when it begins to colour. Pour in 100 ml white wine, allow to evaporate. Cook 400 g spaghetti until al dente, drain and add to the pan. Heat through for 1 minute before pouring the mixture into a serving dish. Top with thin slices of bottarga and finely chopped parsley. (For 4 people.)

Tuna bresaola

More rare, but delicious, pieces of bluefin tuna are salt-cured, then sun-dried. Slice thinly and enjoy in a salad seasoned with olive oil, freshly ground black pepper and lemon, or try it with melon (like prosciutto) or in thin slivers on pasta (like bottarga).

Tuna salami

A ficazza is a sort of large cured sausage made from chopped and seasoned pieces of tuna, with quite a salty flavour. For a salad or pasta dish, it needs to be sliced and dressed with oil and lemon. It also works well with fresh figs.

Nero *di seppia* Cuttlefish ink

This inky-black product is used to colour pasta or rice. It is contained in a little sac that you must not pierce while cleaning the cuttlefish. Be careful as it stains. To make up for this, keep in mind it has a very agreeable flavour.

Ink in sachets

As it's not always easy to find cuttlefish with their ink at the fishmonger's, you can buy ink in sachets. Allow about 2 g per person for colouring home-made pasta or making a sauce.

Canned cuttlefish in ink

These are prepared with onions, tomato, white wine and olive oil. Reheat gently and pour over spaghetti. A little chopped parsley and freshly chopped chilli to garnish and the deed is done. Allow one 280 g can per 2–3 people.

Risotto nero

Add 1 can of cuttlefish in ink (heated), 2 knobs of butter and 2 tablespoons grated parmesan to a risotto 3 minutes before the end of cooking time. (For 4 people.)

Make crostini from grilled polenta and serve them warm with cuttlefish ink sauce.

For purists: home-made cuttlefish ink

You will need 500 g small cuttlefish (maximum 12 cm in length so they are nice and tender). If you can't find any cuttlefish with their ink, add 8 g of sachet ink to the recipe.

Open the cuttlefish using scissors and carefully remove the black ink sac (its colour is superb!). Set aside in a glass.

Remove the intestines of the cuttlefish, cut out the beak (in the middle of the tentacles) and the eyes. Slice the cuttlefish bodies into 1 cm strips and the tentacles into 2 or 3 pieces.

In a large, deep frying pan, gently sauté 1 chopped onion and 1 crushed garlic clove in 5 tablespoons of olive oil. Add the cuttlefish, allow to cook for a few minutes, whilst stirring. Moisten with 100 ml white wine and allow to evaporate before adding 300 g crushed fresh or canned tomatoes. Add 1 tablespoon chopped parsley and freshly ground black pepper. Allow to cook for 20 minutes over low heat.

Meanwhile, pierce the ink sac with scissors, dilute in a little hot water and strain through a fine sieve.

Pour the ink into the sauce and cook for a further few minutes. The cuttlefish must be very tender. If not, keep cooking (for tender cuttlefish, cook on a medium/low heat for 40–50 min). Add a little salt to taste before serving. (For 4 people.)

condiments

Olio extra vergine *di oliva*
Extra virgin olive oil

I adore olive oil and I always have two or three bottles open, all different, which I use depending on the recipe.
I cook everything with olive oil, except egg pasta, ravioli, gnocchi and risotto – I prefer butter for these.

Making your choice

A good olive oil is expensive but it's a very good investment. Always have two varieties of olive oil on hand, one fairly mild variety for everyday use and a fruitier one for big occasions. Some specialist stores offer tastings, so don't hesitate to try and hunt down your favourite.

Extra virgin

Buy oils described as extra virgin, these are made only from olives. The quality depends on the climate, the variety and above all the method of production. Look on the label for the area of production (which is not yet mandatory to display...) and any DOP labels (denominazione di origin protetta) which indicate

Tips

Light, delicate oils, like those from Liguria and Lake Garda, go well with milder-tasting dishes, such as fish. They are perfect for a basil pesto or for giving a crisp texture to a savoury pastry.

Fruity oils with a touch of pepperiness, for example from the hills of Chianti, in Tuscany, lift the flavour of salads and *bruschette*, or use for flavouring (after cooking), soups, minestrones, pasta with tomato sauce, *pasta fagioli* or a simple steak.

The gentle, smooth oils from the south of Italy are ideal for recipes using tomatoes, eggplants, capsicums or tuna. Try to get an oil made with Coratina olives from the Apulia region, with a slightly bitter and fruity flavour.

the food has been officially protected under European Union regulations approved in 1992. The colour is not always an indication of quality.

Au naturel

To appreciate a good olive oil in its pure state, drizzle some on a piece of (good) bread, on a bruschetta with tomatoes or simply dress some spaghetti with oil, garlic, chilli and parsley.

Deep-frying

You can deep-fry with (extra virgin) olive oil, as it tolerates high temperatures well (up to 180°C).

Flavoured oils

Make your own flavoured oils. It's easy and the results are delicious.

For a garlic-flavoured oil, marinate 6–8 peeled garlic cloves (sprout removed) for at least 3 days in a 250ml bottle of olive oil. A practical option, especially for tomato sauces. Use within a short period of time.

For a salad dressing, process the leaves from a bunch of basil or parsley with 100 ml olive oil. Use this mixture within 24 hours.

Aceto **balsamico** Balsamic vinegar

Balsamic vinegar is a blend of aged vinegar and grape must. A great classic that can be found almost everywhere. Its appeal lies in a taste that is both sweet and sour. Watch out, however, for cheap imitations.

Tips for buying

Many good-quality brands of balsamic can be found as long as you're willing to pay a little more. Expect to pay $6 to $60 per 250 ml, depending on the production process and age. Choose vinegars from Modena and Reggio Emilia, without additives or colours (with a maximum of 2% caramel).

Packaging

In some gourmet food stores, you can find balsamic vinegar in spray form, for spritzing on dishes. *Crema di balsamico* can be used for decorating plates like they do in high-class restaurants.

Uses

In a vinaigrette for a salad (rocket and parmesan, for example) or by itself on warm green beans and zucchini. Use it for deglazing white meats or calf's liver, or else to add character to a fresh fruit salad.

The king of vinegars ...

The one with the label 'Aceto Balsamico Tradizionale di Modena' or 'di Reggio Emilia'.

This is a precious condiment made exclusively from cooked grape must (juice). It is a very dark brown and has a syrupy consistency. A few drops are enough to appreciate its strong flavours, which is sweet and sour at the same time, but well balanced. Try it by itself on vegetables (raw or cooked), grilled fish, bollito, etc. Connoisseurs even use it in desserts with ingredients like strawberries, pineapple and vanilla ice cream.

A little history ...

Balsamic vinegar has been known since the Middle Ages for its medicinal qualities. The master tasters explain the traditional production process that accounts for the rarity of this product: 'It ages by a slow process of acetification arising from natural fermentation and gradually becomes more concentrated through a very long ageing process in barrels made from different woods, without the addition of flavouring substances.'

Produced in limited quantities, the balsam is aged for between 12 and 25 years in the attics of Modena or Reggio Emilia. Hence its high price! For a 100 ml vial, expect to pay approximately $100 for a 12-year-old vinegar and $250 for a 25-year-old one! Since 2000, it has enjoyed DOP status.

TARTUFO BIANCO White truffle

The queen of white truffles is the Alba White Truffle, which only grows in Italy. The best comes from the area around Alba, in the Piedmont region, but they are also found in other regions in Italy. Its size varies (from the size of a walnut to the size of an apple) and it has a very intense perfume.

Where to find it

Harvested from October to December, it can be found in many good restaurants. It can also be found at the end of the year in gourmet food stores and on certain food stalls that specialise in rare and expensive produce. It is generally kept dry in rice (which absorbs moisture), and the recommendation is to eat it within a short period of time. It is a luxury item for grand occasions. To take advantage of it throughout the year at a more reasonable price, use white truffle-based products which serve perfectly well as a substitute.

Truffle-based products

Truffle paste, truffle-flavoured butter or oil are products perfect for everyday use. Their strength depends on the percentage of truffle they contain. Adapt the quantity used in a recipe accordingly. To flavour pasta, a risotto or a sauce, blend some truffle paste or truffle butter with a little hot cream. For risotto, mix in this combination at the end of cooking. Truffle-flavoured olive oil is more suited for use in salads. Partner it with pine nuts and parmesan cheese. It is delicious on rocket with bresaola and parmesan cheese.

The other truffles

The black truffle has a more delicate flavour. The best are harvested in winter. It is used grated or pounded using a mortar and pestle and seasoned with olive oil and salt. It stands up well to cooking. Keep it in the refrigerator (maximum 1 week) in a plastic bag that is changed every day. More common but much less flavoursome, the summer truffle (also black) has the virtue of still being relatively inexpensive.

How to use it

Fresh white truffle is eaten raw, to preserve all of its aroma.

To remove any soil just before use, brush under a stream of cold water, wipe dry, then slice very thinly, directly onto your dish.

It is perfect in a risotto with white wine and parmesan cheese, divine on fresh tagliolini with butter or scrambled eggs, ideal for flavouring melted cheese or a cream sauce for ravioli, delicious in a salad of raw porcini mushrooms, exquisite with an escalope of veal with butter, marvellous with a beef carpaccio. It also goes well with pumpkin or anchovies.

Pinoli e pistacchi Pine nuts and pistachios

Crunchy and tasty, these aromatic little seeds go with many sweet and savoury dishes. I like to have some on hand at all times.

Pine nuts

Buy these loose or in packets and always in small quantities as they tend to become rancid. As a result they need to be eaten within a short period of time. Enhance their flavour by toasting them in a dry frying pan.

Uses

Don't hesitate to add them to everything! They are an ingredient in basil pesto but you can also scatter them over your pastas and salads.

My grandmother used them in her pasticcio di magro, a baked pasta dish which contained a handful of pine nuts and raisins and was covered with a layer of béchamel sauce.

The combination of raisins and pine nuts is irresistible, with agrodolce-style sardines, pan-fried silverbeet and escarole (a dish from the south of Italy) or else in caponata (an agrodolce-style ratatouille). For salads, try a mixture of rocket, Pecorino Romano cheese and pine nuts, or else rocket, bresaola, raw zucchini and pine nuts.

Pistachios

Pistachios give your recipes a hint of the East. You can use any flavoursome pistachios, but the ideal is to get yourself some from Bronte, Sicily. This variety grows in the volcanic soil at the foot of Mount Etna and has a sweet and subtle flavour.

Buy them shelled and unsalted for use in cooking. They are sold loose or in packets. Taste if possible to check that they are fresh and crunchy.

Uses

For a crostini topping, chop a generous handful of pistachios and mix with ricotta, a drizzle of olive oil and some pepper. Scatter crushed pistachios over pasta with Gorgonzola and cream, pasta with tuna bottarga, risotto with parmesan cheese and some Prosecco.

Pistachio pesto

A super-practical and delicious product: a mixture of crushed pistachios, olive oil, white pepper and nutmeg. It is sold in jars, ready to use and can be spread on crostini or served with prosciutto or bottarga. For pasta sauce, dilute the pesto with a little of the cooking water then add some ricotta and grilled prosciutto.

Pistachio and rocket pesto

Chop 150 g unsalted pistachios with 30 g rocket, salt, pepper and nutmeg. Add 50 g Pecorino Romano cheese (or parmesan cheese) and 100 ml olive oil and mix until a smooth paste. (For 4 people.)

capperi  Capers

In Italian, the word 'capperi' also means something like: 'That's fantastic!' In any case, this is the exclamation to make when you taste true good-quality capers. The best are grown in Sicily where it is considered very poor form to preserve them in vinegar, as this destroys their aroma.

Packaging

Buy preserved capers in brine or salt, but avoid those preserved in vinegar. Once opened, they keep for a long time in a tightly closed glass jar. Try to obtain capers from Pantelleria or Salina (Sicily), these are the best. The smallest ones have the most flavour. And try caper berries (*cucunci*) for garnishing your salads or served by themselves with drinks.

Caper pesto

For a pasta salad: Rinse 100 g capers and chop with 1 bunch of basil, ½ bunch of mint and 2 garlic cloves. Mix in 50 g grated pecorino cheese (or ricotta salata or parmesan), some chilli and 100 ml olive oil, poured in a thin stream. Then put the pesto in a large bowl, add 6 diced roma tomatoes and 250 g penne pasta cooked *al dente*. Mix together and allow to rest for 30 minutes before eating, adding a little more salt and oil as needed to taste. (For 4 people.)

Uses

The salt should be removed from capers before using. Take the quantity you need from the jar and rinse them under a stream of cold water: they stay salty enough to season your dish. To completely desalt them, soak for 1 hour.

As a condiment, pair them with olives, basil, parsley, mint, lemon, garlic, onions. They are delicious with fish or white meats. For salads, I prefer the small capers and I reserve the larger ones (chopped) for sauces. I often use them in tomato sauces and for dressing pasta or a pizza. As a paste, spread on crostini.

Caper butter

Process a good handful of rinsed capers with a handful of parsley (or oregano) leaves and 80 g butter. Spread this butter on crostini and top each mouthful with half an anchovy.

Erbe Herbs

Garlic, basil, oregano and rosemary are to Italian cuisine what curry leaves are to Indian cuisine. Use without moderation to put a little taste of Italy on your plate. Use fresh herbs if possible. A bunch keeps for a few days in the refrigerator, rolled in damp paper towels inside a plastic bag. If you're afraid you'll forget about them, place them in a glass of water in the coolest spot in the kitchen. For dried herbs, buy organic brands if possible, which have more flavour.

Basil

In Italy, basil is added to everything or just about … for making pesto, of course, but also with summer vegetables (tomatoes, eggplants, capsicums, zucchini), with mozzarella cheese on a pizza, in sauces and salads. Add at the end of cooking and tear it with your hands so it keeps all of its aroma.

Rosemary

For Italians, there is no such thing as olive-oil focaccia, or roast potatoes without rosemary. Chopped or on the branch, fresh or dried, it is ideal for flavouring roast meats or a risotto with parmesan cheese. It is a hardy plant that doesn't need a lot of looking after: try to grow some in a pot on a window sill or in your kitchen.

Sage

Sage has a delicate perfume and an intense flavour. It is used to flavour melted butter for pouring hot over a pasta dish sprinkled with parmesan. The perfect match. It is delicious with veal (saltimbocca), roasts, liver, and also cooked dried beans.

Oregano

Oregano (or marjoram) is better dried than fresh. In the south of Italy, it is almost as common as basil, for adding flavour to tomato salads, pizza, ratatouille or grilled fish. Or crostini topped with sun-dried tomato paste and olives.

Parsley and mint

Parsley is packed full of vitamins. For your Italian recipes, use flat-leaf parsley, as it is the most flavoursome.

It's the basis of the salsa verde for bollito (pot-au-feu). It adds flavour to grilled fish (add together with a drizzle of olive oil), to simple pasta dishes and to pan-fried seafood (mix it with garlic).

Add it as well to spicy sauces (amatriciana, puttanesca) or to your soups (at the end of cooking).

Mint is especially used in the south of Italy. It adds flavour to fried zucchini (marinated or stuffed), broad beans, lamb chops and grilled swordfish. Try it also on a melon salad.

Mostarda

Salsa verde

50 g crustless bread
8 tablespoons red wine vinegar
1 garlic clove
50 g parsley leaves
50 g celery leaves
50 g capers
50 g cornichons
2 hard-boiled eggs
8 anchovy fillets
100 ml olive oil

Moisten the bread with 5 tablespoons of vinegar and let it soak for a few minutes. Then process all of the ingredients together with the oil and the rest of the vinegar.

Mostarda

Mostarda is a piquant preparation made from candied fruits flavoured with mustard oil. The most famous varieties come from the north.

La Mostarda di Cremona is made using (highly coloured) whole fruits, preserved in syrup. It is served with pot-au-feu (bollito).

Mostarda di Mantova uses pieces of quince as its base. More delicate in flavour, it is wonderful with pumpkin tortelli.

Mostarda Veneta (from Veneto) also uses quince as its base, put through a food mill and mixed with citrus peel. Try it with mascarpone on a slice of panettone.

Mostarda is sold in jars. The easiest to find is the Mostarda di Cremona, which is the most pungent. If using as a purée, you can process the fruits with their syrup and adjust the quantity according to your taste.

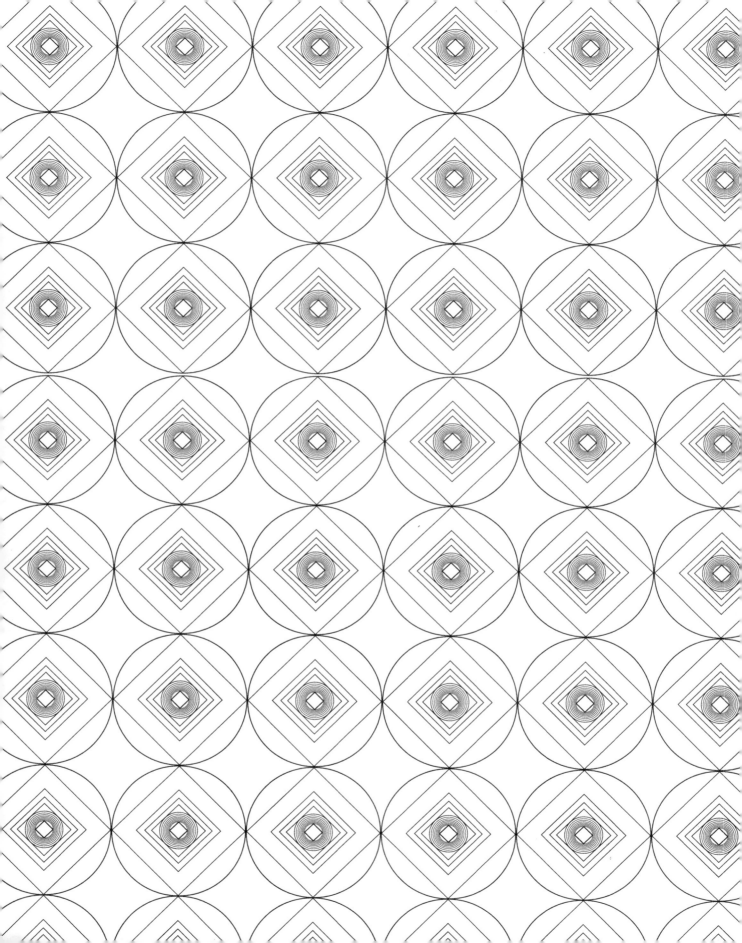

pizza & co.

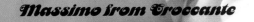
Massimo from Croccante

Mia pizza **Margherita**

For 4 people
Preparation time: 15 minutes
Cooking time: 20 minutes

olive oil
800 g pizza dough (see page 50)
100 g tomme cheese, grated
1 bunch basil
350 g canned crushed tomatoes
200–250 g mozzarella cheese

Preparation

Preheat the oven to 250°C. Grease the baking tray with olive oil. Flatten the dough out with your hands, quite thinly, making a small raised edge so that the topping doesn't fall off. Scatter over the tomme cheese, the basil and the well-drained and lightly salted tomato. Drizzle over some olive oil before putting in the oven. After 15 minutes, scatter the mozzarella, thinly sliced, over the pizza and return to the oven for 5 minutes. The pizza should be golden underneath and around the edges.

The authentic Napolitana

Pizza was born in Naples and it deserves a certification of quality (this is underway). True pizza is a disk of good-quality dough topped with fresh ingredients. The dough is flattened by hand, not with a rolling pin. The edges must be crusty but not the base. It is cut into wedges and eaten with the hands. This is why it shouldn't be too large (25 cm in diameter instead of the overloaded giants found in some pizzerias …).

The topping is quite simple. On a marinara, crushed tomatoes, 1 thinly sliced garlic clove, oregano and olive oil (but no seafood). On a margherita, crushed tomatoes again (the base of a pizza), 80 g mozzarella (fior di latte or buffalo) slices, and just before serving some basil and a drizzle of olive oil is added.

To eat well in a pizzeria, choose a basic margherita (tomato and mozzarella) and ask them to top it with cherry tomatoes and rocket. Add thin slices of Prosciutto di Parma, anchovies, fried eggplant or buffalo mozzarella when the pizza comes out of the oven. Try as well deep-fried calzone, stuffed with mozzarella, ricotta and salami (or ham).

LA PASTA **DI CASA** Home-made pizza dough

It takes a little time but it's the best. Try it out in any case, even if just to relieve your stress with some intense kneading! Or try ready-made pizza bases for a quick and easy alternative to making your own dough. For the topping, improvise depending on the season. Beware though of creating over-complicated combinations: true pizza is a masterpiece of simplicity.

For 800 g dough
Preparation time: 20 minutes
Resting time: 2 hours 20 minutes

500 g (strong baker's) flour
3 level teaspoons salt
25 g fresh yeast
250 to 300 ml lukewarm water
1 teaspoon sugar
3 tablespoons olive oil

Preparation

Make a mound of the flour with a hollow in the centre and scatter the salt around the edges. Mix the yeast with the water, add the sugar and allow to rest for 15 to 20 minutes. Pour this yeast starter into the hollow of the flour, with the olive oil. Knead the dough with your hands for 10 minutes, adding a little water if necessary. The dough must be very pliable. Shape into a ball, draw a cross on top with the point of a knife and cover with a cloth. Leave to rise for 1 to 2 hours. It needs to double in size. For a successful rise, cover the dough with a damp cloth and leave it in a warm place (between 25 and 30°C, near the oven or a heater) and sheltered from draughts.

Serving *ideas*

Without topping

This is the pizza bianca, served instead of bread. It is eaten with Italian charcuterie products or cut into wedges for dipping in a very good olive oil by way of a pre-meal snack …

Cheese

Over the dough, before adding the tomatoes, scatter 3 heaped tablespoons of grated parmesan cheese. At the end of cooking, add 250 g mozzarella cheese (drained for 10 minutes beforehand) or 300 g mild cow's milk tomme cheese. For a four-cheese version (without tomato), top each quarter of the pizza with a different Italian cheese: mozzarella, Gorgonzola, ricotta, fontina, taleggio, parmesan …

Olive

Top the pizza with small pieces of tomato mixed with small capers (barely rinsed) and a handful of pitted and chopped black olives. Add 1 tablespoon oregano and a drizzle of olive oil. Five minutes before the end of cooking, you can top with mozzarella cheese or desalted anchovies.

Vegetable

On a base covered with a layer of tomato pulp, add fresh diced tomato that you have marinated beforehand with a little oil, crushed garlic and basil. Add a handful of rocket just before serving. Using the same base, top with grilled vegetables marinated in oil (eggplant, zucchini, capsicum) or eggplant deep-fried in olive oil.

Salami

On a margherita pizza, when it comes out of the oven, scatter over 4 slices prosciutto (Parma or San Daniele) and a few leaves of rocket. Using the same base, midway through cooking, add some very good ham, roughly torn into pieces by hand.

Fried pizza

Fry mini-pizzas (7 cm in diameter) in oil (olive or peanut) and top with a spoonful of tomato sauce with basil.

FOCACCIA

Focaccia is a sort of thick pizza bianca with olive oil. It has a crusty surface, is soft inside (and above all not rubbery). It should appear glossy with olive oil (it is sprinkled over the dough before baking).

My focaccia recipe

For 8 people
Preparation time: 30 minutes
Resting time: 2 hours 30 minutes
Cooking time: 20 minutes

600 g (strong baker's) flour
3 teaspoons salt
25 g fresh yeast or 7 g dried yeast
300 ml lukewarm water + 5 tablespoons
1 tablespoon sugar
200 ml olive oil + 6 tablespoons
1 tablespoon sea salt

Preparation

The preparation is the same as for pizza dough. Make a mound of the flour with a hollow in the centre and scatter the fine salt around the edges. Mix the yeast with the 300 ml water, add the sugar and leave to rest for 20 minutes, then pour this starter into the hollow of the flour with the 200 ml olive oil. After kneading, the dough should be quite pliable. Shape into a ball, cut a cross into the top, cover with a cloth and leave to rise for about 2 hours in a warm place, sheltered from draughts.

Using a fork, beat the rest of the oil with the 5 tablespoons water and the sea salt (it will dissolve a little). Work the dough for 1 minute before spreading it out on a well-oiled baking tray, pushing it outward from the centre using your hands. Try to get it all the same thickness. Use the tips of your fingers to make little hollows in the dough, brush with half of the oil mixture and leave to rest for 10 minutes. Cook the focaccia for 20 minutes in a preheated 240°C oven. The top should be golden. Coat with the rest of the oil mixture when it comes out of the oven.

Flavouring ideas

You can add 200 g pitted and halved taggiasca olives, 2 tablespoons rosemary or 1 small handful of chopped fresh sage. Just before baking the dough, you can add a topping of 2 onions, sliced into very thin rings.

For a richer version, incorporate some diced mild cheese (some stracchino for example) into the dough. You can also, quite simply, serve the focaccia cooked with the same cheese.

Serving ideas

You can serve focaccia with drinks, cut into cubes, plain or filled with vegetables, cheese, or salami products.

As an accompaniment to meals, serve it plain or flavoured with small black olives, rosemary and/or onions. You can also use it to make sandwiches.

Piadina **romagnole** Italian flatbread

This is a soft, round flatbread (like traditional unleavened bread), made from wheat flour, water, oil and salt. Depending on the recipe, it can be made using lard instead of oil, milk instead of water and sometimes baking soda or yeast.

It was traditionally served as bread for the peasants of Romagna, its region of origin. They cooked it on earthenware hotplates, today replaced by iron or cast-iron griddles. The piadina romagnole sold in shops is very good; it's thus quite rare to go to the trouble of making it at home ... It just needs to be reheated before being filled.

Packaging

Piadina romagnole is sold vacuum-packed (it can be kept in the fridge for a few days) and it is ultra-thin (so it doesn't take up much space). It can be filled according to taste with prosciutto, cheese and/or vegetables.

Ideas for fillings

A mild cheese (stracchino or squacquerone) and a few leaves of rocket.

The classic trio of mozzarella cheese, tomato and basil (or rocket), even if the Romagnols don't much like their dish being turned into a pseudo-pizza ...

Italian charcuterie products, ham, Prosciutto di Parma, culatello, porchetta, coppa, mortadella, salami ... In Romagna, they even fill them with fresh sausage.

Grilled vegetables, semi-dried tomatoes and a few leaves of rocket. For a complete meal, you can add some cheese or charcuterie products.

The recipe for piadina

You will need 1 kg flour, 150 g lard or 100 ml olive oil, baking soda, salt and enough water to bind the ingredients (add it gradually).

Combine the ingredients to obtain quite a stiff dough. Flour a rolling pin (not too much) and make quite thin rounds of dough. Cook the piadina in a very hot cast-iron frying pan (or a smooth hotplate), pricking the bubbles that form on the surface with a fork. Eat straight away.

ttobre : mortadella et
naigre balsamique 2,5

vembre : speck,
rescenza et aubergine
rillée   5

cembre : Parma,
rmesan, rucola ,5

assico : Parma,
ozzarella de buffle
tomate   .5.5

PIADINA

Giugno : pecorino
doux, tomates sechées,
laitue et huile   4
Luglio : Aubergines
grillées, courgettes,
poivrons, oregan et 4.5
vinaigre balsamique
Agosto : thon aux herbe
tomates, laitue 5.5
Settembre : mozzarella
de buffle, jambon bla
vinaigre balsamique 5.

PIADIN

Gennaio : salame
provola et huile
Febbraio : jambo
crescenza, artich
Marzo : tomates
parmesan et sa
piquant

Take-away piadina at Croccante

PANINI

What you buy in France under the name of 'panino' (a semi-cooked pseudo-baguette filled with various ingredients and vaguely waved under a griller) has absolutely nothing to do with its Italian counterpart. And while it's an inexpensive hot meal for poor students, it's nevertheless a shame it bears the same name as an infinitely tastier product.

My favourite fillings

A good panino (the singular form of panini) is made to order, with ciabatta-style bread, and eaten straight away to get a mouthful of all of its different flavours. If you make it in advance, beware of ingredients that yield a lot of moisture: drain slices of mozzarella cheese for at least 10 minutes and use sun-dried or semi-dried tomatoes rather than fresh.

Salami

Prosciutto (Parma or San Daniele), buffalo mozzarella cheese, rocket and a drizzle of olive oil.
Culatello.
Ham or prosciutto and pistachio pesto.
Porchetta, rocket, sun-dried tomatoes or olive paste.
Bresaola and artichoke hearts marinated in olive oil or bresaola, fresh goat's cheese (caprino) and a mixture of fresh herbs.
Mortadella di Bologna, thickly sliced, or coppa. You can also add marinated artichoke hearts or an olive paste.
Speck (preferably paired with a black bread), butter and some gherkin.

Cheeses

Try out all the different flavours, from the most delicate to the most intense. By itself or paired with other Italian specialties, cheese adds flavour to any panini.

A great classic, tomato and buffalo mozzarella cheese, with plenty of basil or oregano and a drizzle of olive oil.
Taleggio cheese and rocket or Taleggio and speck.
Scamorza cheese (which has a smoky flavour), sun-dried tomatoes and rocket.
Gorgonzola cheese, walnuts and diced celery or pear.
Stracchino cheese and rocket.

Vegetables

Grilled eggplant, tomatoes, basil and mozzarella cheese.
Grilled capsicum or sun-dried tomatoes, tuna in oil, chopped capers, oregano.
Grilled zucchini, mint and Pecorino Romano (a sheep's milk cheese).

Grissini

Grissini, lingue or ciappe are all fabulous products which can replace bread and are perfect when you're waiting for dinner. They store well for long periods of time so you can keep them in bulk at home. If you have trouble finding them, pressure your supplier to order them in for you.

Grissini

These are long sticks made from flour, water, yeast and sometimes a little lard or olive oil. Traditional Piedmontese grissini (rubatà) are shaped by hand. They are light and very flavoursome, much better than the industrially made version.

Serving ideas

Grissini can be served with drinks alongside antipasti (try a slice of Prosciutto di Parma rolled around a grissini stick). Offer them with salads, charcuterie products or a cheese assortment. Try as well the grissini flavoured with rosemary, olives or walnuts.

Taralli

These are round, crunchy, ring-shaped biscuits. A specialty of Apulia in Italy, these are made from flour, dry white wine, local olive oil (or lard), salt and various flavourings. They are cooked in boiling water then baked in the oven. They are available in both savoury and sweet versions. The best have the aroma of olive oil and are flavoured with fennel seeds, chilli, oregano or dried onion. Perfect to serve with antipasti, they satisfy those peckish moments during the day.

STUZZICHINI AL MAIS
Grissini al mais

Ingredienti: Farina di grano tenero tipo 0,
farina di mais 9%, olio di oliva 9%,
sale, lievito naturale, malto
Prodotto naturale senza conservanti aggiunti

Prodotto per SERVICEPAN S.p.A.
Via Roggorini 7, Borgosesia VC
Ne stabilimento di via Aighe Desio, 516 milano

Scad. 30/04/2006   gr. 150 €
Lotto 3805

Grissini

Piedmontese lingue crispbread

These are my favourites! Something like a flattened-out grissini, 10 cm wide and 50 cm long. Thin, crispy and tasty, you can buy them in boxes, sealed in plastic bags so that they don't go soft.

Serving ideas

Use instead of bread, and with drinks. Break them up into small pieces and spread them with olive paste, or top them with sun-dried tomatoes or very creamy cheeses (Gorgonzola, stracchino, ricotta …).

Recipe for home-made lingue

For about ten lingue, you will need 500 g flour, 2 teaspoons salt, 250 ml lukewarm water and 5 tablespoons olive oil plus a little extra oil for brushing.

Combine all of the ingredients and knead the dough for at least 5 minutes. Cover and leave to rest for 20 minutes in a warm place. Divide the dough into ten pieces, then shape each into long (30 cm) rectangles with a rolling pin. Brush them with oil and bake them in the oven at 200°C. Take out the lingue when they are golden.

Ciappe

These close relatives of lingue come from Liguria and have the delicious aroma of the region's olive oil. They are thicker than lingue and less imposing in size. They are eaten plain (like bread) or with generous toppings with drinks.

Pane carasau

This Sardinian bread, which is also called carta da musica (sheet music), is very thin, very flat and very crunchy. Like an old parchment … Made from wheat semolina, water and salt, it used to be the bread eaten by shepherds. It is sold in packets of several rounds, carefully packaged (it is very fragile).

How to serve it

Serve plain in place of bread or with a topping with drinks. Reheat it in the oven, season with salt and a drizzle of olive oil.

Broken into pieces, add to a salad of fennel and orange, or tomatoes and onions.

A more novel use is to soak it for a few minutes in hot stock to soften and use it like sheets of lasagne, filling it with vegetables and cheese.

BRUSCHETTA E CROSTINI

Bruschetta

Pronounced 'broosketta'. The base is a generous slice of toasted bread, rubbed with garlic and drizzled with a very good olive oil (young and peppery). Then, it can be topped any way you like ... This light, pleasant meal is eaten just about everywhere these days — at a beach-side kiosk, in a bar with drinks, in a restaurant or at home.

What kind of bread?

A good country-style bread with a dense crumb that's toasted at the last minute so that it stays crunchy. Serve hot preferably.

Ideas for toppings

My favourite is bruschetta with Lardo di Colonnata (see opposite).

Highly aromatic, it melts in the mouth. Allow one slice of Lardo per person.

Bruschetta with tomatoes is a summer classic. A very simple and delicious dish. Choose tomatoes with flavour! You can crush them in your hands directly onto the bread, with a little basil. If you have a little time, peel some tomatoes (they just need to be boiled for a few seconds to remove the skin), seed them, chop into small dice and allow them to drain for 30 minutes in a strainer with some salt. Season with olive oil, slivers of garlic, basil or oregano. Leave to marinate for a further 30 minutes. Toast the bruschetta, rub with garlic, drizzle with olive oil and add the marinated tomatoes. You can add well-drained cubes of mozzarella cheese or combine the tomatoes with rinsed salted capers, pieces of black olive, chopped anchovies and basil.

For a vegetable bruschetta, combine grilled eggplant, zucchini and capsicum marinated in oil and sliced into thin strips, season with olive oil, salt, pepper and fresh herbs (mint, basil or parsley). Add a few drops of balsamic vinegar.

Crostini

These little slices of toasted bread, the diameter of a baguette, are generally served with drinks. You can use bread with sesame or poppy seeds, black bread (dense) or wholegrain. Serve in the same way as bruschetta, topped with vegetables or spread with olive paste or sun-dried tomatoes. Also delicious with Salami products, artichoke hearts and cheese. They are eaten using your fingers.

Crostini with Lardo di Colonnata (at Da Rosa)

formaggi

FORMAGGI Cheeses

If the whole world has already adopted the now famous parmesan and mozzarella cheeses, mascarpone, ricotta and Gorgonzola are also on their way to becoming indispensable items. But did you know that there are a great many Italian cheeses? Italy boasts a significant production of around 450 cheeses and each of its regions has its specialties. Discover them during a trip to Italy, or at your local Italian delicatessen, letting yourself be guided by the DOP label (the Italian equivalent of the French AOC). Here's a short tour of Italy to encourage you to taste our best cheeses.

Piedmont offers one of the widest selections. There you will discover the rare and legendary Castelmagno cheese, a member of the veined-cheese family, the flavoursome Bra cheese, the tomme cheeses, the intense square-shaped Raschera cheese, or else the Robiola cheeses from the Langhe, some versions flavoured with black truffle that are made from a blend of cow's, sheep's and goat's milk. Easier to find: Fontina and Fontal cheeses, mild and delicate, delicious melted, and the ricotta-style Seiras cheese.

In Lombardy, a region of high mountain pastures and flat plains, the cheeses to try are Bagoss cheese, nicknamed the 'grana' of Brescia, the smooth mountain cheeses Bitto and Quartirolo, a skimmed-milk cheese. Easier to find: the sharp and tasty Provolone Val Padana cheeses, and of course the Taleggio, Crescenza, mascarpone and Gorgonzola cheeses.

Trentino-Alto Adige, a region influenced by Austrian traditions, is renowned for its mountain cheeses: the ones to try are Vezzena, very tasty, the mild and delicate Dobbiaco and of course the Grana Padano Val di Non.

In Veneto, discover Ubriaco, a semi-fresh or ripened cheese, its flavour developing in the grape must of noble grape varieties (its rind takes on the colour of wine) and Monte Veronese cheese, fresh, ripened or mature. Easy to find in shops: Asiago, which can be a mild semi-cooked cheese or sharp and hard, and Piave, the cheese never missing from the table.

In Friuli there are the various 'latteria' farmhouse cheeses to enjoy, including the first-rate Montasio cheeses, made from cooked semi-skimmed cow's milk, cylindrical in shape and sold young, with a quite mild taste that becomes pleasantly sharp and tasty when ripened. Gnocchi or pasta is fantastic with grated 'Carnica', a smoked ricotta cheese.

In Emilia-Romagna, you can join in the worship of Parmigiano Reggiano as well as the Formaggi di Fossa which, in accordance with an ancient recipe, is ripened in pits dug out of the volcanic rock!

In Tuscany and the central regions, the majority of the cheeses are made from sheep's milk, including the various pecorino cheeses. Try also the briefly ripened cacciotta (tomme-style) cheeses, fresh and mild.

In the south (Molise, Campania and Apulia), the sheep reign in the mountains and the buffalo in the marshy areas (hence mozzarella!). There is the renowned Caciocavallo Silano cheese, the most typical of the ripened, stretched-curd cheeses. On the sharp side and lending itself well to frying (see scamorza), is the Canestrato Pugliese, a ripened sheep's milk cheese with a sharp taste, as well as the exquisite ricotta cheeses of different ages.

In the south of Basilicata, Calabria, Sicily and Sardinia, arid and dry areas where only sheep and goats are reared, we find pecorino cheese, the rare Caciocavallo Podolico cheese, or else the rectangular-shaped Caciocavallo Ragusano.

Parmigiano **Reggiano** Parmesan cheese

Part of my family comes from Reggio Emilia, one of the most food-loving regions of Italy, and above all the homeland of Parmigiano Reggiano. I remember my grandmother, when she visited us at Treviso, always brought us an enormous piece of Parmigiano cheese. I grew up with this cheese and I cannot manage without having a good piece in the house at all times, like the majority of Italians for that matter.

The quality

Parmigiano is sold from 12 months of age, but acquires greater aroma and flavour at 24 months and can be aged for up to three or four years. The straw-yellow interior and flaky texture (the cheese breaks off in slivers) are synonymous with quality. The mountain variety that comes from the high pastures of the Appenine mountains in Emilia, and the 'red cow' variety, from an almost extinct breed, are the most sought after.

How to buy it

Ask your cheese vendor to cut a block of parmesan cheese for you (200 g minimum). I would advise

Parmigiano crisps

In a hot, non-stick frying pan, put a heaped teaspoon of grated Parmigiano, and make a round with a diameter of about 8 cm (make it easier for yourself by putting the Parmigiano inside a smooth round pastry-cutter). Spread the cheese out until it is 2 or 3 mm thick and sear quickly on both sides, using a spatula to turn them around. You can shape these crisps, while they're still hot, into tuiles (a cylindrical shape) or containers (on the base of a small round bowl). You can also make these in the oven on baking paper, 4 to 5 minutes at 180°C, keeping a close watch on the cooking!

Shortcrust pastry with Parmigiano

For making biscuits to serve with drinks or for small tarts with a 'richer' taste. Once cooked (barely golden), fill with a thin layer of ricotta cheese and semi-dried tomatoes or pan-fried zucchini. The ingredients for the pastry: 125 g butter, 100 g grated Parmigiano, 2 egg yolks, 250 g flour.

against buying packets of ready-grated parmesan cheese: it has already lost most of its aroma. In any case, pre-packaged, grated parmesan is not something that even exists in Italy! Keep your block of parmesan in the refrigerator, covered with plastic wrap or a damp cloth so that it doesn't dry out.

The king of cheeses

Serve with drinks or at the end of the meal: using a parmesan knife (or a large knife point), cut (irregular) bite-sized pieces. Serve them with good grissini and delicious with a few drops of traditional balsamic vinegar.

Pastaresa

This is a recipe from my Aunt Edvige from Reggio Emilia, for a soup that's simple but full of flavour!

Mix together on the work surface 150 g grated Parmigiano with 100 g breadcrumbs (home-made, if possible!), 2 whole eggs and 1 yolk, salt and a pinch of nutmeg, until you obtain a compact mixture. Grate it roughly or shape small lumps with your hands on a floured surface. Let the dough 'dry', then cook it for a few minutes in stock. (For 4–6 people.)

Grana Padano

The hard cheese par excellence. It has the same appearance as Parmigiano Reggiano: with a milder and more delicate taste, ideal for serving with drinks or at the end of a meal, try it with some Mostarda di Cremona, with aromatic honeys flavoured with thyme or peach, with walnuts and hazelnuts.

Where is it produced?

Lombardy, Veneto, and the provinces of Piacenza and Cuneo (DOP label). The renowned 'Val di Non' Grana Padano (DOP), rich and intensely flavoured, comes from the high-altitude Trentino mountains. About four million wheels of Grana Padano are produced every year.

The difference

The same raw materials are used to make Grana Padano and Parmigiano Reggiano: raw milk, an injection of whey and calf rennet. The difference is in the ripening period (which is only 15 months for Grana) and in the diet of the cows.

Experiment

Try sharp-tasting relishes: red onion or green tomato, ideal for an aged 24-month Parmigiano, which is quite mild. For a 3-year-old Parmigiano, serve instead with a sweeter preserve, a pumpkin jam for example, or – why not? – a chilli jam.

Pecorino

The sheep's milk cheese, of which there are several varieties, from different regions.

The most well known: Pecorino Romano

Percorino is a cheese made from whole sheep's milk, aged for 8 to 10 months. Despite its name, it is mostly produced in Sardinia (DOP label). It is a cooked cheese, hard and quite dense, with an intense, pungent flavour. It is ideal for grating. It is often used in place of Parmigiano in the cooking of the central-south region of Italy and is unique in pasta all'amatriciana in Rome (see sauce recipe, page 156) or in spaghetti cacio & pepe (with pecorino cheese & pepper).

Cook 400 g spaghetti until al dente. Meanwhile, melt 150 g Pecorino Romano cheese over a gentle heat in a little olive oil, combine with the pasta and season generously with freshly ground black pepper, adding a little cooking water if necessary. (For 4 people.)

The other Pecorinos

Pecorino di Pienza

This is one of the best varieties of pecorino cheeses from Tuscany. There is a semi-mature variety recognisable by its red rind or a mature variety with a black rind. It can be served with drinks on a mini-kebab with fresh grapes, in a salad of baby leaves with toasted pine nuts or at the end of a meal with honey or a fruit jam.

Pecorino Maremmano

Originally from Tuscany, it has a milder and more delicate taste than the other varieties of pecorino. It is eaten fresh or semi-mature.

Pecorino Sardo

Enjoy this mature but mellow cheese with bilberry (or perhaps a blueberry) jam.

Fiore Sardo (DOP) is a hard, very tasty cheese.

Pecorino Siciliano

Pecorino Siciliano (DOP) is eaten very fresh or very mature with peppercorns; a red fruit jelly will bring out its piquancy.

Mozzarella *di bufala* Buffalo mozzarella

It's hard to imagine summer without mozzarella. For me, it is synonymous with freshness, and memories of holidays in the south. On the beach in Apulia, at lunchtime, people would have a small braid of fior di latte mozzarella in one hand and cherry tomatoes and a piece of focaccia in the other … and I learned to do the same thing myself: true pleasure. Natural flavours, full of taste!

Buffalo in Italy?

Buffalo mozzarella cheese comes from a species closely related to the cow that came from South-East Asia around 500 AD and adapted well to the marshy areas in Campania and Latium. They say that the best buffalo mozzarella is the one that's made and eaten on the same day, as its taste changes from hour to hour. What then to make of mozzarella brought from 2000 km away. Cow's milk mozzarella, also called *fior di latte*, is a soft cheese and comes in different shapes: a ball, braid (treccia), small ball (bocconcini) or cherry (ciliegia). The denser cheese, brick or ball-shaped, is an industrially made product.

Plain, to immerse yourself in its different aromas. With good tomatoes, basil and a drizzle of olive oil. With prosciutto from Parma or San Daniele, a few Taggiasca olives, semi-dried tomatoes, rocket leaves and traditionally made grissini; or else chopped into small dice in a pasta salad with tomatoes marinated with garlic, basil and olive oil.

Mozzarella and a refreshing salad of fennel with olive oil.

Mozzarella and fresh figs (cut perfectly ripe figs into 1 cm slices and serve them topped with a slice of mozzarella and seasoned with hazelnut oil).

Mozzarella and a salad of melon and tomatoes with olive oil and balsamic vinegar.

Mini-kebabs of cherry mozzarella with a vegetable (cherry, semi-dried or sun-dried tomatoes, or wrapped in grilled eggplant, capsicum or zucchini), with in all cases a leaf of basil or good oregano.

And the quality?

If you want to taste a real good-quality mozzarella cheese, you need to track down a good supplier (a good Italian delicatessen or a good cheese shop) and ask what day the precious Mozzarella di Bufala Campania comes in, it's much better eaten within 48 hours … The same criteria of quality apply when choosing *fior di latte* mozzarella: it's the freshness that counts, and of course the traditional know-how, guarantee of peerless taste. Eat it as soon as possible, at room temperature.

Crumbed mozzarella

Cut into ½ cm slices (if using buffalo mozzarella, drain it for 10 minutes) or 5mm then, dip in flour, seasoned beaten egg and breadcrumbs. Fry in hot olive (or peanut) oil on both sides, until golden in colour. Place on paper towels before enjoying them sprinkled with oregano, along with a salad of tomato, basil and bulb spring onion, for example.

Crostini

Spread small slices of bread with butter, add a small slice of mozzarella, thin slices of tomato, half a rinsed anchovy fillet, pepper and oregano. Bake in a preheated 180°C oven for 6 to 8 minutes.

Burrata, provola e scamorza

Burrata mozzarella

Although it's now renowned, burrata cheese, from Apulia, has only been made since the 1930s. Burrata is a pouch of stretched-curd cheese enclosing a mixture of fresh cream and cow's milk mozzarella. It's a true delight!

It is sold wrapped in the leaves of a local plant or the rush plant, and absorbs their pleasant aromas. As with buffalo mozzarella, it must be eaten within 2 to 3 days (check when buying, or when ordering in a restaurant!).

Enjoy plain with good grissini. For a novel ravioli or fine lasagne filling, you can process it with a little cream, salt and pepper, and accompany with finely diced black olives and semi-dried tomatoes. Burrata is also surprisingly delicious with mandarin marmalade and rye bread.

Provola & scamorza

These cheeses are similar to stretched-curd cheeses like mozzarella and are sold fresh after ripening for about 10 days, smoked or unsmoked. The smoked version is more distinctive and tasty. Once opened, keep them covered with a damp cloth and eat within 10 days.

How to use them

With drinks

Make mini-kebabs from cubes of scamorza (or provola) cheese and sun-dried tomatoes.

Grilled cheese slices

Cut into 1 cm slices and grill for 30 seconds on each side. Serve very hot with a tomato and rocket salad: a true indulgence!

With vegetables

You can also serve them with grilled capsicum or eggplant.

As an ingredient

Five minutes before the end of cooking, add some finely diced smoked scamorza cheese and chopped rocket to a basic risotto (onions, white wine, stock).

Add flavour to your pan-fried chicken breasts by covering them with a thin slice of scamorza cheese and rounds of pan-fried zucchini, then put in the oven to brown.

Sebastiano (at Cisternino)

RICOTTA

I'm a big fan of this dairy product! It is derived from whey that is cooked twice: hence the name 'ricotta' (re-cooked). For Italians, it's an all-purpose product, a bit like crème fraîche for the French. I always have some in my refrigerator; preferably buy the fresh, soft ricotta with a grainy texture sold by your Italian grocer. Ricotta is a seasonal spring or autumnal product, with a similar taste to the fresh Provençal cheese brousse or the Corsican brocciu. Fresh ricotta should be eaten within 24 hours.

How to use it

Ricotta can be used from starter to dessert: I would say it is used as a base to make a dish more subtle. Try it mixed with mascarpone, goat's cheese or grated Parmigiano, depending on the desired flavour.

Quick ideas

Spread on crostini with vegetable or dried fruit pastes to soften the taste or make it more subtle (olive, sun-dried tomato or grilled capsicum pastes, basil, rocket, walnut, pistachio or walnut pestos).

Mix ricotta in equal proportions with mascarpone, flavour with truffle oil and garnish with pine nuts.

Ricotta can be used in place of a béchamel sauce, simply dilute it with a little cream or milk. Try it also in baked pasta dishes, pasta al forno (see recipe, page 160).

Ricotta and spinach or silverbeet are a perfect couple, but you may also use ricotta and artichoke or zucchini as a filling for savoury tarts and crêpes, lasagne, ravioli, vegetables or gnocchi.

For savoury tarts, you can replace the cream and egg mixture with 250 g ricotta, 1 or 2 eggs, 80 g parmesan cheese, salt, pepper and nutmeg. Pour into your tart base, top with your choice of vegetables and it's ready to go into the oven.

My mother's ham and ricotta feuilleté

Use a rectangular baking tray or a 26 cm round tin. Take two pieces of pure butter, flaky pastry or a light olive oil tart pastry. Roll out thinly. Spread the ricotta/egg/parmesan mixture on one of the sheets using a spatula, add 150 g finely chopped ham and cover with the other sheet. Brush with an egg yolk beaten with a little water and bake on high heat for 30 to 35 minutes.

Ricotta + sugar

Fresh ricotta is delicious for breakfast, spread on bread with acacia honey or bilberry jam.
Use to fill rich shortcrust pastry tarts or Sicilian cannoli. For a light tiramisù, replace the mascarpone with (strained) ricotta.

Ricotta for grating

The hard, salted sheep's milk variety of ricotta is very tasty. It is ideal for grating on pasta and salads. Use ricotta instead of parmesan in summer.

Smoked ricotta

Fresh or matured, smoked ricotta has a subtle and aromatic taste. Sold vacuum-packed, once opened it should be kept in plastic wrap in the refrigerator.

Mascarpone

Since the year 2000 this cheese has been available everywhere. Why is it so abundant? Because you need mascarpone to make tiramisù (one of the most popular desserts overseas!).

Real mascarpone

Creaminess is the main quality that is notable in commercially made mascarpone – when it comes to flavour, it is not very interesting if eaten on its own. Commercially made mascarpone is nothing compared to fresh, traditionally made mascarpone, which has an incredibly fine and rich taste. It is found in shops in Italy from autumn to spring but it must be eaten within 48 hours. To give the more authentic taste of the 'fresh' version to a commercially made tub of mascarpone, add two heaped tablespoonfuls of (traditionally made) crème fraîche.

Quick ideas

Mascarpone is used in the same way as butter or crème fraîche to soften flavours and add creaminess.

It and other cheeses (ricotta, fresh goat's cheese, Gorgonzola): add flavoured oils and garnish with toasted sunflower seeds. Serve on crostini, lingue, celery sticks, or on slices of baked root vegetables (a real treat) – parsnip, turnip-rooted chervil, yellow carrot, etc.

Mascarpone and truffle-flavoured oil and anchovy paste (quantities according to your taste): spread on crostini and garnish with small, rinsed, salted capers or oregano.

Mascarpone and hot soups: mix into the soup cold before serving, allow 1 heaped tablespoon of mascarpone for 2 people.

Mascarpone and pasta sauces: blend the mascarpone with a few spoonfuls of the pasta cooking water.

Mascarpone and risotto: to 'mantecare' the risotto (make it creamy), add cold mascarpone at the end of cooking, instead of or in combination with butter (1 tablespoon for 2 people), for vegetable risottos rather than those with fish.

Mascarpone and hot, soft polenta: it gently melts on top (or underneath)!

Sauce for smoked fish

Process 200 g cooked fennel (steamed or boiled) with 8 tablespoons olive oil until you obtain a thick emulsion. Add 2 tablespoons of balsamic vinegar, salt, pepper, 150 g mascarpone then enough of water to make a liquid sauce (ideal with swordfish, tuna or smoked salmon). For 4–6 people.

For dessert

I used to eat fresh, traditionally made plain mascarpone with my fingers and lick them clean! I don't do that with the commercially made version …

Dessert creams

The simplest way: combine the mascarpone well with an equal quantity of ricotta (depending on your diet) and a little milk (if you want a thinner consistency).

Add your favourite flavourings (mine: lemon and/or orange zest, cinnamon, ginger, orange flower or saffron), sweeten with icing sugar or honey.

Mascarpone and eggs: if you add eggs you will have the cream for making the legendary tiramisù. This cream is also fantastic with strawberries, red berries and baked figs.

GORGONZOLA

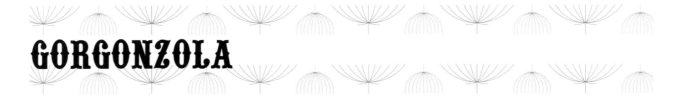

Gorgonzola

A good, soft and very creamy Gorgonzola is a real indulgence. This veined cow's milk cheese is a favourite in northern Italy, its place of origin (from Lombardy and part of Piedmont).

Buying

It is sold wrapped in foil for the best preservation of its qualities. Look for Gorgonzola that is nice and creamy and you will not be disappointed.

With drinks

It's an essential basic item. Fill a celery stick with a Gorgonzola-mascarpone mixture or a lovely witlof leaf (with a few centimetres trimmed from the base, to make an elegant mouthful) topped with a few toasted pine nuts.

Or try a large Gorgonzola crostini: just out of the oven, hot and creamy, scattered with nuts.

It goes very well with salads of witlof, celery or pears. Their crunchy texture and fresh taste provides a good contrast to the creamy texture of the cheese.

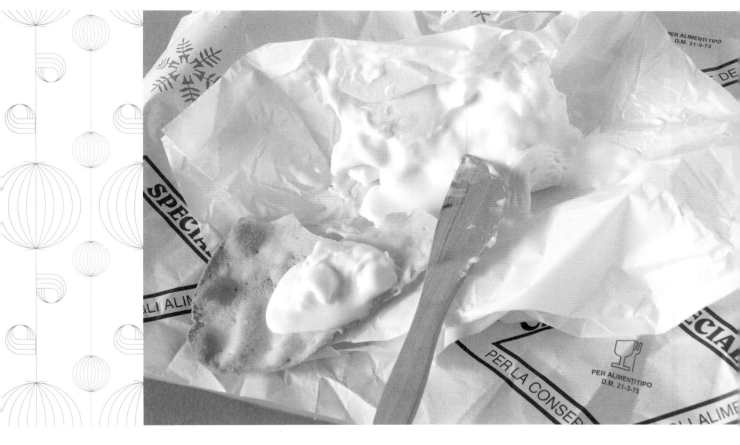

Taleggio

A very well known soft cow's milk cheese from Lombardy. It is enjoyed for its strong, penetrating taste as well as its double texture, both soft around the edges and dense in the middle.

You can recognise it by its square shape and rosy exterior but ensure you don't eat the rind.

Stracchino & Crescenza

Which is to say: creamy and delicious cheeses!

I am a great fan of these two cheeses with their milky taste. The soft, creamy, delicate, stracchino (pronounced strakkino) was, in effect, the cheese of my childhood along with parmesan and ricotta. It is my Proustian madeleine – I eat it melted into creamed vegetables or spread on bread.

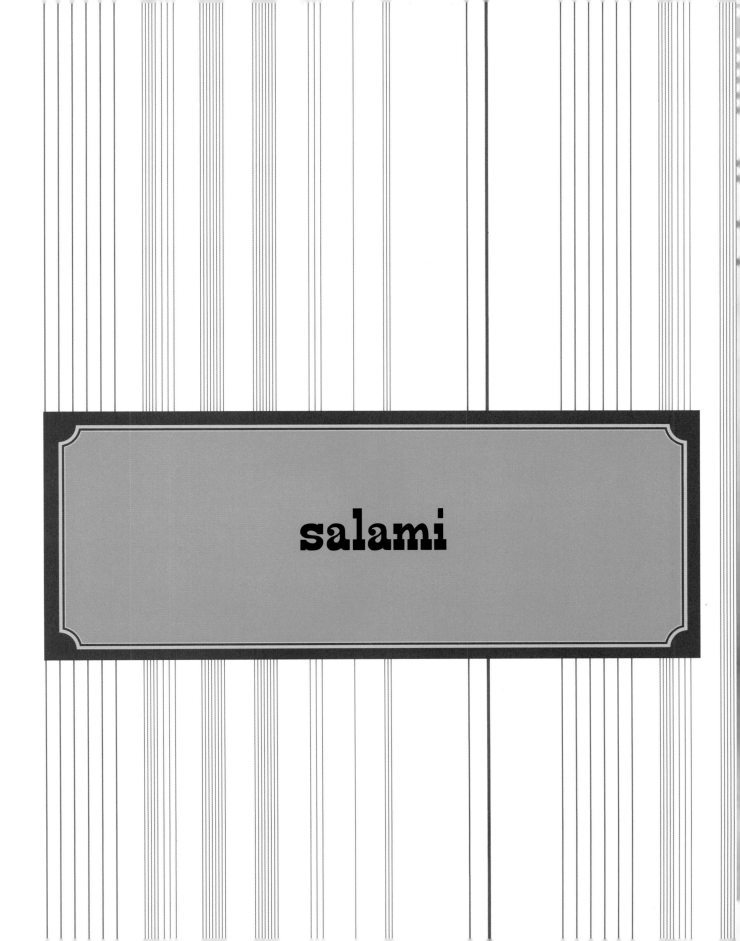

salami

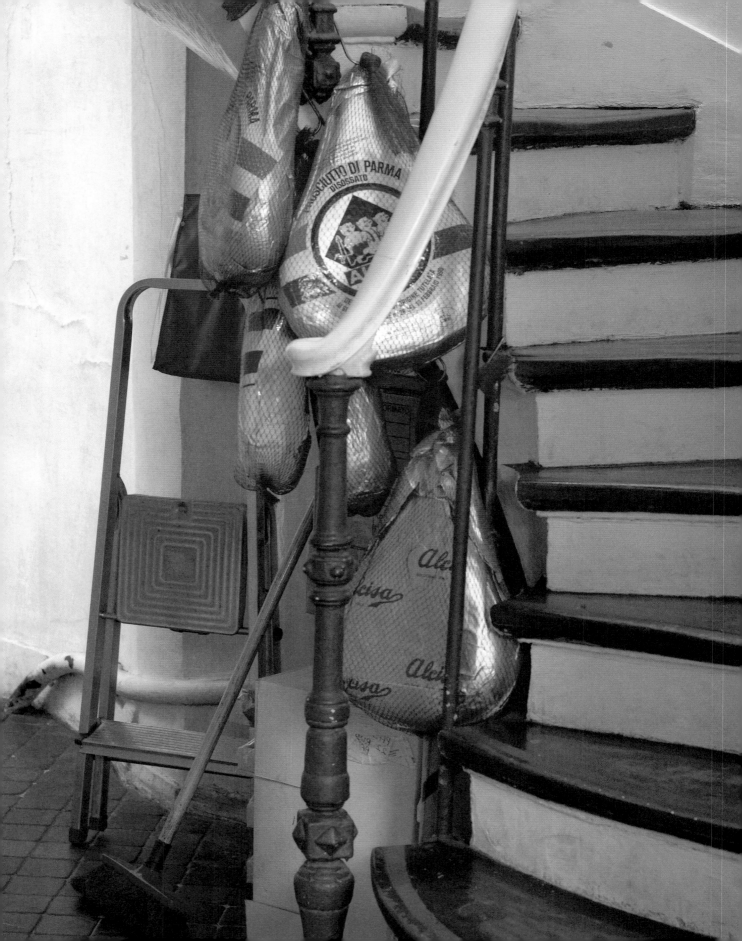

Prosciutto crudo

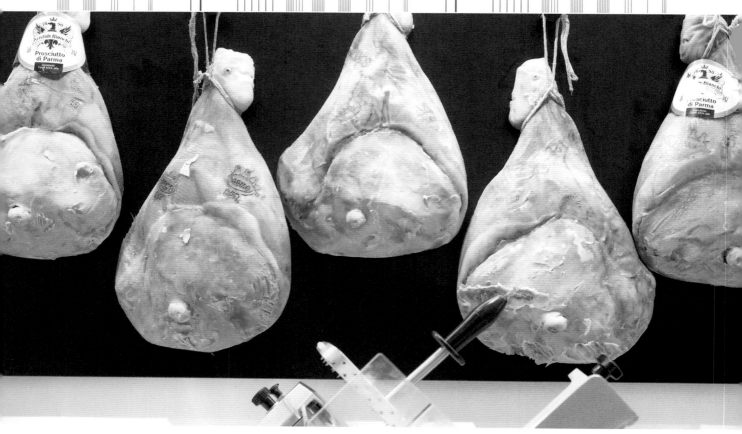

How to buy it

Parma or San Daniele, that's the dilemma ... Both of them aim to be smooth and subtle. To choose, find out their level of maturity: the older they are, the more flavour they have. Prosciutto di Parma is sold from the age of 18 months and up to 30 months. The San Daniele version is sold at 12 months but is said to be better at 16 months. Check also what part of the ham the slices are cut from. At the beginning they are a little dry, at the other end very moist. Choose prosciutto that is labelled, with the name printed on the rind, and specially marked as traditionally made.

Prosciutto from Parma is produced in Emilia-Romagna, and the San Daniele variety in Friuli. The same breed of pig is used for both, the same curing process which uses salt exclusively. The difference is the result of the particular climate and traditions. In Parma, for example, the animal is fed on parmesan whey.

My suggestions

Here's a good basic: a plate of prosciutto (4 slices), 125 g buffalo mozzarella cheese, a few leaves of rocket dressed with olive oil and balsamic vinegar, semi-dried tomatoes, black olives and grissini.

In summer, serve good-quality prosciutto with melon, a great classic, as long as your ingredients are very fresh. It's what makes the difference ... You can add a handful of rocket dressed with olive oil and balsamic vinegar. Serve on a plate or on mini-kebabs with drinks. In the same spirit, you can also try the combination of prosciutto and well-ripened fresh figs. It's a more interesting contrast if you choose one of the saltier prosciuttos (from Tuscany, for example).

A quick and sumptuous recipe

Pan-fry 100–150 g finely chopped prosciutto with a knob of butter, add 200 ml pouring cream and allow to reduce a little. Then mix in 2 tablespoons of basil – or pistachio nut – pesto and 1 handful of toasted pine nuts. Mix through tagliatelle and don't forget to add the parmesan cheese on top. To chop prosciutto without turning it into mush, harden the slices in the freezer before slicing them. (For 4 people.)

The cut

In Italy, prosciutto is sold in quantities of 100 g: not by the number of slices. Expect to get between six and eight slices for 100 g, or a serving for one person as a one-dish meal, otherwise for two.

Ask your supplier to keep at least 1 cm of fat and to slip plastic between each slice so they separate more easily.

How to serve it

The prosciutto should be sliced in front of you and eaten within the day, or else its flavour is no longer the same. But you can still sauté it and serve it finely diced on pasta.

Prosciutto from Parma and San Daniele does not really need any accompaniment. Serve it on a plate with grissini or some bread, and perhaps a few drops of very good balsamic vinegar.

Mortadella

This is a traditional Salami product from Emilia-Romagna. The most renowned is the mortadella from Bologna.

Authentic mortadella is made from lean pork meat and some fat. It is seasoned with spices, including peppercorns. It must show an 'S' (for suino, 'pork') printed on the outside. Beware of imitations that use other kinds of meat, powdered milk, egg whites and artificial flavours.

The giant

Mortadella is simply a very large sausage where the minced meat is put into a casing and cooked in temperature-controlled ovens. The larger it is, the slower it is cooked, and the tastier it is. It is found in very good delicatessens and sliced by hand …

The taste

Mortadella has a unique flavour, it is well balanced and lightly spiced. In traditionally made versions, the colour may be a darker pink (it doesn't contain any antioxidants).

How to serve it

There are the fans of the thick slice (3–4 mm), hand-cut if possible, and those of the very thick slice (1.5 cm), cut into dice, and the devotees of the thin machine-cut slice. It also all depends on how you are using it.

With drinks, serve cubes of mortadella with pieces of Grana Padano (or parmesan) cheese and serve with picks.

When cooking, chop it up to flavour tortellini, a polpettone (meatloaf) or meatballs made from white meats.

The Davoli brothers

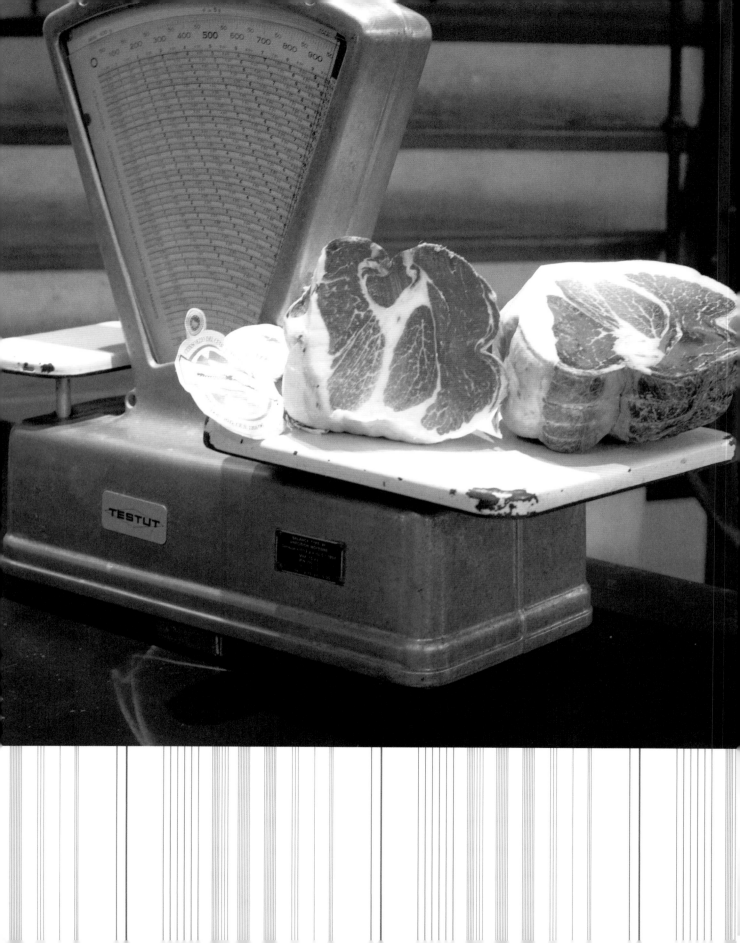

CULATELLO

The king of hams, from a very ancient tradition ...

The difference between culatello and prosciutto

To make culatello, the bone and rind is removed from a pork thigh to leave just the buttock muscle (hence its name), the leanest and most prized part. The flesh is massaged with salt, pepper and garlic, then wrapped in the pig's bladder to form a pear shape. The humid climate of the plains in the south of Parma provides perfect conditions for maturing, which lasts for almost a year.

How to buy it

In theory, before slicing culatello, it should be rinsed and left to marinate for three days in red wine to tenderise it. Check whether this has already been done but it will still be good even if not.

It's an expensive ham, but an exceptional product. The most renowned comes from Zibello.

How to serve it

Take the time to enjoy and make the most of it! You can enjoy it in a panino, a piadina, a focaccia or on a pizza.

Two slices are enough for a delicate starter. Serve with rocket and parmesan cheese and dress with oil and balsamic vinegar.

Serve finely shredded on pasta very simply prepared with French shallots sautéed in butter, rocket leaves and slivers of parmesan cheese.

Pancetta **e coppa**

The curing of pancetta (pork belly) or guanciale gives a more intense flavour to dishes, with less calories than butter or olive oil!

Pancetta

Pancetta is the pig's belly. The most well known are pancetta affumicata (smoked), pancetta arrotolata (rolled) and pancetta stesa (flat). There are also regional variations, such as Pancetta Piacentina (seasoned with spices), Pancetta di Calabria (hot) and from Trentino (with garlic).

Pancetta affumicata

Before being smoked, the pancetta is sprinkled with spices, herbs, salt and pepper (it is not rolled). The taste is quite mild, especially if it is traditionally made product. It is used in cooking to enhance the flavour

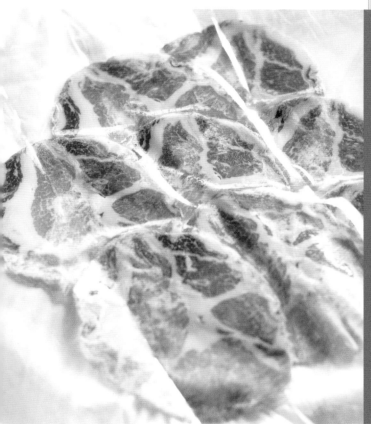

Coppa

Coppa can be recognised by its cylindrical shape, a beautiful red colour streaked with white and pink. It is made from the muscles of the pork neck, and seasoned with salt and pepper. There are also versions with garlic and white wine (Parma) or spices (Piacenza). It is called capocollo in the southern regions (where it is usually stronger and quite spicy).

How to serve it

With drinks, on mini-kebabs with fresh figs or artichoke hearts in oil.

In a panino with a green or black olive paste.

With an assortment of Salami products and antipasti (black and green olives, capsicums, artichokes, dried tomatoes).

On pasta dressed with a rocket pesto. Slice very thinly.

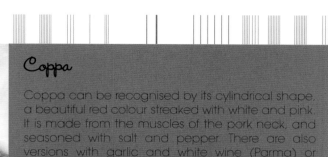

of sauces and to wrap around fillets of fish (monkfish) or white meats.

Pancetta arrotolata

Pancetta arrotolata is tender and flavoursome. It is used to wrap lean meats before cooking (to prevent them from drying out) or browned in a pan to give flavour to vegetables, meat stuffings and sauces.

Pancetta stesa

Produced in the middle of Italy, pancetta stesa is often flavoured with garlic and fennel. It has quite a strong and salty taste. You can use it to flavour sauces or omelettes. Its matured version (pancetta stesa stagionata) is much more tender and delicate.

Lardo

Il guanciale

Guanciale is salted pork cheek, matured for two months. In Latium, it is flavoured with pepper, garlic, sage and rosemary. It is sometimes used for sauces (amatriciana (see recipe, page 156) or carbonara), although pancetta is often used instead, as guanciale can be difficult to find.

Lardo di Colonnata

Colonnata (near Carrara) is the native land of marble ... and lardo. This product was out of fashion for a long time, but it is making a strong comeback with fine-food lovers.

Production

Lardo is made from pork back fat, cut into regular pieces and rubbed with a mixture of salt, freshly ground black pepper, garlic, rosemary and sage (each producer has their own flavouring secrets). The pieces of lard are then stacked in marble basins

How to serve it

Lardo is best eaten by itself to appreciate its sweetness and subtlety. Thinly sliced (2 mm), it melts in the mouth! You can serve it on toasted bread with a pinch of rosemary or plain tomatoes.

to mature in cellars. After six months (or even more), they are tender and very aromatic.

It's a very old method of conservation, and quarry workers were already eating it in the time of Michelangelo (who was himself a big fan).

How to store it

If you buy a whole piece of lardo, wash the salt off the upper part and fold the rind over the already-cut section to avoid it drying out. Store in a damp cloth and keep in a cool, dark spot or in the bottom of the refrigerator.

Lardo di Arnad

The village of Arnad, in the Aosta region, gives its name to a true gourmet delicacy. The pigs are reared on vegetables and chestnuts. The lardo is flavoured with garlic, rosemary, sage, bay leaf, cloves, juniper berries, nutmeg, cinnamon, yarrow … It is eaten in the same way as Lardo di Colonnata. Try it on rye bread spread with chestnut honey.

Salami

Porchetta

Porchetta is a 7 kg suckling pig, seasoned with salt, pepper, garlic and herbs (rosemary or wild fennel). It is cooked for 3 hours in a 300°C oven, which melts the fat and results in an almost lean meat. The recipe has hardly varied since Roman times but today the meat is boned, rolled and tied to make lovely slices.

Serving ideas

Use to fill a panino or piadina and enjoy with rocket, olive paste and sun-dried or semi-dried tomatoes. Arranged on a plate served with salad and grissini.

Speck

Speck is a smoked and boned mountain ham, made for centuries near Bolzano, in Alto Adige. The pork leg is salted and spiced (pepper, garlic, juniper, chilli) then smoked for three weeks. The maturing process takes several months to a year.

How to serve it

Its delicately smoked flavour goes well with butter. In the mountains, it is enjoyed with rye bread with fennel seeds, butter and cornichons.
Serve it with drinks, with sottaceti (baby onions, carrots, capsicum and cornichons pickled in vinegar) or olives. It is also delicious with grilled polenta.

Fresh pasta with speck

Cook 400 g pasta (penne, orecchiette or tagliatelle) until *al dente* and flavour with 100 g speck, cut into strips and browned in 70 g butter. Sprinkle with grated parmesan cheese. (For 4 people.)

Bresaola

Bresaola is a real treat, made from raw beef, salted and spiced (pepper, herbs, spices, wine, each producer has their own recipe). It is then matured for between three and six months. Ideal for dieters as it is high in protein and has almost no fat. When it's good quality and well stored, it's succulent!

How to choose

Ask for bresaola that comes from Valtellina (Piedmont), subtle, aromatic and moist. It is a beautiful bright red, but above all not dark (this means it has been cut for a long time).

How to serve it

Like carpaccio or prosciutto, in thin slices (1 mm thick) with olive oil, lemon juice and freshly ground black pepper. Depending on your mood, try a few variations by adding rocket and shavings of parmesan cheese, very thin rounds of raw zucchini, white truffle-flavoured oil and toasted pine nuts. Marinate it for 10 minutes with herbs. With drinks, serve on a mini kebab with artichoke hearts in oil or fruit segments (grapefruit, apple, peach …).

Stuffed bresaola rolls

For 12 slices of bresaola, use 150 g of a creamy cheese (mascarpone and ricotta or fresh goat's cheese) mixed with two handfuls of chopped fresh herbs (chives, parsley, basil, chervil …). Make rolls or little parcels secured with a chive or a strip of leek.

Salsiccie **E SALAME** Sausages & salami

Another area where abundance reigns ... Depending on the particular climate and traditions, you will find a large number of specialties, each more aromatic than the last ... In the north, sausages (luganega) are often seasoned with pepper, cinnamon, garlic and white wine. They are cooked fresh. In central Italy, the preparation is simpler (salt and pepper) and they are eaten dried. In the south, they are flavoured with fennel or chilli and eaten fresh or dried.

Fresh sausages

These are succulent simply pan-fried and served with hot polenta. Add slices to a risotto or pasta, with sautéed French shallots or leeks. Not forgetting the parmesan cheese.

Salami

The most well known is Milanese salami. It is produced all over Italy, using finely chopped pork or beef. It is the basic all-purpose filling for panini.

Neopolitan salami is the most spicy and flavoursome. Ideal for serving with drinks and with grissini.

The little salamis alla cacciatora (hunter's salami) can be slipped into a pocket, school bag or picnic basket. They are dry, with a dense texture and are very practical for satisfying small cravings.

Renowned for its quality, salami from Felino (near Parma) is both moist and delicate.

The best products

Salame d'oca or goose salami, which can be served hot with mashed potato. Today it is sometimes made with pork.

Wild boar salami (il cinghiale), is a gourmet delicacy from Tuscany that's very flavoursome with a gamey taste. Still from Tuscany, try la finocchiona, a salami seasoned with fennel, with small pieces of meat.

Ciauscolo (from the Marche region) is an exceptional product, with a very smooth interior that can be spread on bread.

Sopressa Vicentina is a noble salami from Veneto, seasoned with spices and herbs. Its flavour is delicate and peppery, its texture moist. You can eat it by itself, with bread or grilled polenta, or you can cook it in a sauce.

Sopressata

This is also called coppa di testa. This is a dry sausage made from the tail, tongue and cartilaginous parts of the pig. It is flavoured with spices and lemon and orange zest. Delicious with country-style bread or vegetables.

Prosciutto cotto

This is the Italian name for cooked ham (usually just 'ham' in English). It is flavoured with herbs, sometimes smoked (praga). You can also find plain ham, ideal for Italian-style toast.

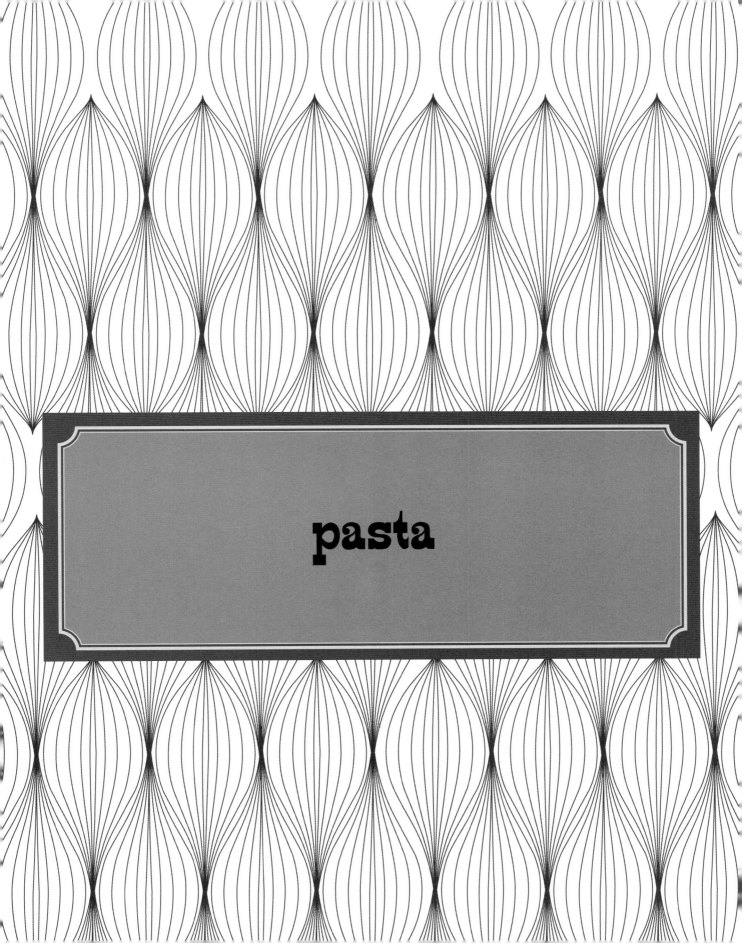

pasta

Pasta fresca **all'uovo**

Fresh egg pasta

To successfully make fresh pasta, you need to take the weather into account. The air should be quite humid in order to keep the pasta supple and elastic. Lasagne, ravioli and tagliatelle are specialties from the north of Italy, while the south is the homeland of dry pastas.

My fresh egg pasta recipe for lasagne, ravioli, etc

The basic recipe is made using flour and eggs. Salt is optional. I like to add a little oil and milk to the dough.

For 6 to 8 serves of ravioli,
10 serves of lasagne, 6 serves of tagliatelle

500 g flour
1 pinch salt
5 eggs
1 tablespoon olive oil
1 or 2 tablespoons milk

For a firmer dough, replace one-third of the flour with the same quantity of fine durum semolina.

Get the eggs and milk out of the refrigerator ahead of time: the ingredients need to be at room temperature to successfully form a smooth mixture.

To make the dough

Place the flour and salt on the work surface, make a hollow, break the eggs into it and mix with a fork. Incorporate the flour little by little, working with the fingertips. For a quicker method, you can use a mixer.

Work the dough on the work surface, kneading it for 10 minutes using the heel of your hand. Add a little flour at regular intervals. When the dough becomes smooth and shiny and small air bubbles form, roll it into a ball. Let it rest for 30 minutes to 1 hour (2 hours if you have the time) at room temperature, wrapped in plastic wrap.

To roll out the dough

Working the dough with a rolling pin is an art in itself, one handed down from generation to generation. The thickness is not always very even, but the pasta holds sauce better. Take the equivalent of 2 'eggs' of dough, flatten into a round and roll with a rolling pin, always starting from the centre. You need to work fairly quickly, or else the dough may dry out. (In Emilia-Romagna, the room is humidified by keeping a large pot of water boiling on the stove.)

If you really love home-made pasta, it is worth investing in a pasta machine. Always work with small quantities (the rest of the dough should be kept in a plastic bag, so it doesn't dry out). Flour the dough before feeding it into the machine, opening the rollers to their widest setting. Then fold it in half or thirds before feeding it into the machine to obtain a thin sheet. For stuffed pastas, avoid flouring the pasta at the end of the process.

For lasagne

Feed the dough several times through the rollers or roll it out using a rolling pin, making quite wide sheets. Arrange them on a cloth so they're not touching each other.

I prefer to pre-cook sheets of lasagne: the taste is better and they don't dry out as much when they are baked. Drop them into boiling salted water with 1 tablespoon olive oil added for 2 or 3 minutes, no more than three or four sheets at the same time, or else they may stick together. Place them straight away in a large bowl of cold water to stop the cooking process, drain and spread them out on a clean cloth without overlapping them.

If you buy ready-made lasagne sheets, opt for fresh ones.

For tagliolini, tagliatelle, pappardelle

If you don't have customised rollers, roll the sheets of pasta up to cut them across: ½ cm for tagliolini, 1 cm for tagliatelle, 2 cm for pappardelle.

Unroll the pasta and make into a nest on a cardboard tray with holes in it (so that the air can circulate). Cover and keep them away from humidity. Cook them within two days.

Cooking fresh pasta

Allow 1 litre water and 10 g coarse salt for every 100 g pasta. You can add 1 tablespoon olive oil to the water but I only do this for lasagne. The other pastas don't stick if you stir them regularly.

The cooking time depends on the size of the pasta. Take care with fresh pasta, which cooks very quickly: stay close by. I never look at my watch and rely only on my sixth sense. When I think that it's almost right, I take a piece of pasta out of the water, hold it between my fingers to judge its suppleness and taste it: it needs to be al dente, which is to say, firm to the bite.

You can add a glass of cold water before draining to stop the cooking process. Reserve a little of the cooking water to extend the sauce if necessary.

Butter or cream?

Fresh egg pasta goes well with butter. In Italy, cream is rarely used, as it masks the flavour of other ingredients. But if you wish to use it on your pasta, choose pouring cream, which is better than the UHT varieties. Avoid crème fraîche, which adds a sour note. In any case, you won't find any in Italy: what is sold there under the name *panna fresca* is pouring cream.

Tagliatelle *al ragù*

Bolognese sauce

For 6 people
Preparation time: 20 minutes plus
30 minutes soaking time
Cooking time: 1 hour

For the sauce

25 g dried porcini mushrooms
100 g carrot
100 g onion
100 g celery
250 g beef (chuck)
250 g veal (shoulder)
100 g prosciutto
1 tablespoon olive oil
40 g butter
200 ml red wine
250 ml hot vegetable stock
1 bouquet garni (thyme, rosemary, bay leaf)
400 g canned tomatoes
salt, pepper

700 g fresh tagliatelle
60 g butter
100 g parmesan cheese

Preparation

Soak the porcini mushrooms for 30 minutes in lukewarm water. Chop the vegetables, meat and prosciutto into small pieces. Sauté them for 20 minutes in the oil and butter. When the mixture starts to stick, moisten with the wine, and allow to evaporate over high heat.

Season with salt and pepper, add the mushrooms, roughly chopped, their strained soaking water, the hot stock and the bouquet garni. Cover and allow to simmer for 40 minutes. Halfway through the cooking, add the tomatoes.

Cook the tagliatelle in a large pot of boiling salted water. Allow to cook for 3 to 4 minutes after they return to the boil, then drain. Put them straight into a large bowl with the butter, pour over the ragù and serve without delay with grated parmesan. Season with salt and pepper to taste.

If you're in a hurry

Chop the vegetables in a food processor and use coarsely minced meat. However, the sauce is better if the ingredients are chopped with a knife.

Ragù in bianco

Use only veal and replace the wine with dry marsala and 750 ml stock. Leave out the tomatoes.

My suggestion

Make a large quantity of sauce. You can serve it with gnocchi or lasagne. If there is some left over, freeze it.

PAPPARDELLE AL RAGU D'ANATRA

Pappardelle with duck ragù

For 6 people
Preparation time: 15 minutes
Cooking time: 1 hour

For the ragù

1 duck, quartered
1 tablespoon olive oil
100 g chopped carrot
100 g chopped onion
100 g chopped celery
2 garlic cloves, crushed
2 good-sized rosemary sprigs
150 ml dry white wine
500 ml stock
400 g canned tomatoes
salt, pepper

700 g fresh pappardelle
60 g butter
100 g parmesan cheese

Preparation

In a large saucepan, brown the pieces of duck skin side down, in the olive oil. When the meat turns golden, discard the fat.

Add the vegetables, garlic and rosemary. Allow to cook for 10 minutes. Pour in the wine and allow to evaporate on a high heat. Add the stock and the tomatoes, season with salt and pepper. Cover and allow to simmer for 45 minutes on a gentle heat.

When the meat is cooked, remove the skin and bones and chop into small pieces. Return these to the saucepan. Add a little extra stock if the sauce is very thick.

Cook the pasta in boiling salted water, allowing it to cook for 3 to 4 minutes once it comes back to the boil. Drain and mix with the butter in a large dish. Pour over the ragù and serve with grated parmesan cheese.

If you're in a hurry

Make the ragù with a roasted, boned and pre-cut duck. Reheat the meat quickly in the cooked vegetables.

Variation

You can also use the ragù to make rolled or baked lasagne. Black olives can be used in place of the tomatoes.

Tagliolini al ragù **di coniglio**

Tagliolini with rabbit ragù

For 6 people
Preparation time: 30 minutes
Cooking time: 40 minutes

For the ragù

1 rabbit, weighing about 1.2 kg
500 to 750 ml vegetable stock
30 g butter
2 onions, chopped
1 tablespoon olive oil
2 garlic cloves, crushed
1 rosemary sprig
1 bay leaf
sage, marjoram and fresh thyme
150 ml dry white wine
3 tablespoons tomato passata (puréed
    tomatoes) with basil
salt, pepper

700 g fresh tagliolini
60 g butter
100 g parmesan cheese

Note

Ask your butcher to bone the rabbit for
you but to give you the bones. You may
need to order this in advance.

Preparation

Cut the rabbit meat into small pieces. Heat the stock in a large
saucepan with the bones from the rabbit (to add flavour). Melt
the butter in a frying pan and brown the rabbit meat for 3
minutes.

In a separate saucepan, sweat the onions with the olive oil and
3 or 4 tablespoons of stock. Allow the liquid to reduce before
adding the meat, garlic and herbs. Moisten with the white
wine. When it has evaporated, add the passata and cover with
the strained stock. Season with salt and pepper. Finish the
cooking on a very low heat (30 minutes).

Cook the tagliolini in a large amount of salted boiling water
allowing it to cook for 3 to 4 minutes after it has come back to the
boil. Drain and place in a large bowl with the butter and mix. Add
the ragù and serve with grated parmesan.

Variation

Add a pinch of saffron threads to the sauce to give it more
flavour.

Tagliolini

In Piedmont, these are called *tajarin*. They are long, narrow
ribbons which go well with rabbit. For a quick dish, combine them
with butter, parmesan cheese and white truffle shavings, which
you can replace with truffle paste mixed with a little stock. Simple
but exquisite.

Maltagliati al ragù d'agnello

Maltagliati with lamb ragù

For 6 people
Preparation time: 30 minutes
Cooking time: 45 minutes

For the ragù

400 g lamb knuckle (hind shank)
2 red capsicums (peppers)
1 onion
2 tablespoons olive oil
30 g butter
2 garlic cloves, crushed
3 bay leaves
100 ml dry white wine
salt, pepper
300 g tomatoes, peeled and diced
100 to 200 ml vegetable stock

700 g fresh maltagliati
60 g butter
100 g parmesan cheese

Preparation

Chop the meat, capsicums and onion into 1 cm dice. In a saucepan, heat the oil with the butter and gently soften the garlic and bay leaves (without allowing them to burn). Add the meat and brown on a high heat for 10 minutes. Add the wine. When the liquid has evaporated, season with salt and pepper, then add the tomatoes and 100 ml of the stock. Cover and simmer for 30 minutes.

In a frying pan, gently sauté the capsicum and onion with 1 tablespoon of olive oil. Add them to the meat mixture 10 minutes before the end of cooking. If the ragù is very thick, add a little stock. Keep warm.

Cook the pasta in boiling salted water, allowing it to cook for 3 to 4 minutes after the water returns to the boil. Drain, mix with the butter in a large bowl, add the ragù and serve with grated parmesan cheese.

Variation

Maltagliati (literally 'badly cut') are irregularly shaped pasta. Roughly tear up thin sheets of fresh pasta. You can use tagliatelle instead.

TAGLIATELLE AI FUNGHI

Tagliatelle with mushrooms

For 6 people
Preparation time: 45 minutes
Cooking time: 30 minutes

For the sauce

1 kg wild mushrooms (extra quantities of porcini,
    chanterelles, black trumpets)
3 tablespoons olive oil
3 garlic cloves
salt, pepper
1 bunch parsley, chopped

700 g fresh tagliatelle
60 g butter
60 g parmesan cheese

Preparation

Clean the mushrooms by scraping them with a knife to remove any soil. Plunge them into clean water twice, taking them out again straight away, and wipe dry. Cut the larger ones into two or three pieces.

In a non-stick frying pan, heat 1 tablespoon of the oil and butter with 1 whole garlic clove. Add the porcini mushrooms and allow them to cook on a high heat without stirring so that they give up their moisture. Season with salt and pepper, add a little parsley and allow to cook for a further 3 minutes over a low heat. Place the porcini in a large bowl (discard the garlic). Repeat with the chanterelles and the black trumpets. Combine the mushrooms with the rest of the parsley. Keep warm.

Cook the tagliatelle in a large saucepan of boiling salted water. Drain and return to the saucepan, add the butter, half the parmesan cheese and the mushrooms. Mix together. Serve in hot plates with the rest of the parmesan.

Variation

Make this recipe in autumn, using wild mushrooms. Otherwise, use a combination of dried mushrooms and fresh cultivated mushrooms. Strain the soaking water and add it to the sauce. Cook it a little longer to evaporate the liquid.

lasagne

Lasagne con porro
e proscuitto di parma

Lasagne with leeks & Prosciutto di Parma

For 6 to 8 people
Preparation time: 1 hour
Cooking time: 50 minutes

For the béchamel sauce
50 g butter
50 g plain (all-purpose) flour
400 ml milk
400 ml hot stock
salt
whole nutmeg, grated
150 g parmesan cheese

For the filling
5 to 6 leeks
2 tablespoons olive oil
40 g butter
8 good-sized slices of
   Prosciutto di Parma (about 200 g)

400 g lasagne sheets

For the topping
20 g butter
50 g parmesan cheese

Preparation

Melt the butter, add the flour and mix well. When the flour begins to colour, pour in the milk little by little while stirring, to avoid lumps. Add the hot stock. Allow to thicken for 10 minutes after it comes to the boil. Season with salt and nutmeg. Remove the saucepan from the heat to add the parmesan cheese. Allow to cool.

Chop the white part of the leeks into small pieces. Soften them in the oil and 20 g of the butter, stirring frequently. Finely dice the prosciutto and brown separately on a gentle heat in the remaining butter.

Cook the lasagne sheets. Drain them well before laying them out on a damp cloth.

Butter a baking dish, cover the base with lasagne sheets, cover with sauce before adding a third of the leeks and a third of the prosciutto. Repeat twice, finishing with a layer of lasagne. Sprinkle over the parmesan cheese and a few pieces of butter. Brown in a 180°C oven for 30 minutes. Rest for 5 minutes before serving in thick slices.

Lasagne arrotolato con carciofi

Rolled lasagne with artichokes

For 6 to 8 people
Preparation time: 1 hour 30 minutes
Cooking time: 1 hour

For the filling

6 to 8 small roman artichokes
1 lemon
3 tablespoons olive oil
2 garlic cloves, crushed
100 ml dry white wine
2 or 3 sprigs marjoram
salt, pepper

For the béchamel sauce

80 g butter
80 g plain (all-purpose) flour
500 ml milk, plus extra 50ml to dilute
salt, grated nutmeg
100 g fontina cheese
100 g parmesan cheese
100 g gruyère cheese
200 ml pouring cream
300 ml chicken stock
400 g lasagne sheets
1 egg white, lightly beaten

For the topping

50 g parmesan cheese, grated
50 g butter

Preparation

With a knife, remove 2 cm of the top of each artichoke, cut the stalks and discard the toughest leaves. Cut the artichokes in two to remove the choke. Chop them further into small pieces, squeeze a little lemon juice over to prevent discolouration and sauté them gently in a frying pan with the oil and garlic. Moisten with the wine, add the marjoram, salt and pepper, and allow to cook for 5 minutes. You can add a little stock so that they don't stick. The artichoke pieces should remain firm.

For the béchamel sauce melt the butter, add the flour and blend well. Allow it to colour before pouring in the milk little by little. Stir constantly or else the sauce will become lumpy. Allow to thicken for 10 minutes, season with the salt and nutmeg. Off the heat, add the diced fontina, parmesan and gruyère. Allow to cool.

Cook the lasagne sheets.

Lay two or three sheets out side by side, with their edges overlapping by 2 cm; glue the edges together with some egg white. Spread a layer of béchamel sauce on the pasta (reserve some for the base) add the artichoke mixture and grated parmesan. Roll the pasta sheet in plastic wrap and place in the fridge so it firms up: it makes it easier to cut it into slices.

Butter a large dish, cover the base with the remaining béchamel sauce diluted with the extra milk, add the lasagne sliced into thick (4 cm) sections, scatter the parmesan and a few pieces of butter over the top. Brown in the oven for 15 minutes at 180°C.

My suggestion

Choose fairly wide sheets of pasta (this will avoid having to put together several sheets) or make small rolls. This also works as a classic-style lasagne (in layers).

Rolled lasagne **with artichokes**
the film ...

LASAGNE CON PESTO E RICOTTA

Ricotta and pesto lasagne

For 6 people
Preparation time: 1 hour
Cooking time: 30 minutes

For the filling

400 g ricotta
1 cup basil pesto
1 egg
100 g pine nuts
100 g parmesan cheese, grated
40 g butter

400 g lasagne sheets

Preparation

Mix together the ricotta, pesto (reserve a generous tablespoon for finishing the dish), egg and pine nuts (dry-roasted in a frying pan).

Cook the lasagne sheets. Drain them well before laying them out on a damp cloth.

Butter a large baking dish, cover the base with sheets of lasagne, cover with the ricotta mixture and sprinkle over the parmesan. Repeat several times. Finish with a layer of lasagne and spread with the reserved pesto. Top with a few pieces of butter before placing in a 180°C oven. Cook for 30 minutes. When it comes out of the oven, wait 5 minutes before dividing it up into servings. Serve with a fresh tomato sauce.

My suggestion

As a change from the big lasagne dish, make the recipe in a cake tin. Reduce the cooking time by 10 minutes and wait 10 minutes to cut the lasagne into slices. The presentation of this version is more appealing.

Lasagne verde *alla bolognese*

Spinach lasagne with bolognese ragù

For 6 to 8 people
Preparation time: 1 hour 30 minutes
Cooking time: 1 hour 30 minutes
  to 2 hours

For the bolognese ragù
25 g dried porcini mushrooms
100 g carrot
100 g onion
100 g celery
250 g beef (chuck steak)
250 g veal (shoulder)
100 g sausage meat
100 g prosciutto
1 tablespoon olive oil
40 g butter
200 ml red wine
salt, pepper
250 ml beef stock
1 bouquet garni (thyme, rosemary, bay leaf)
2 cloves
400 g canned tomatoes

For the béchamel sauce
70 g butter
70 g plain (all-purpose) flour
1 litre milk
salt, whole nutmeg

400 g spinach lasagne pasta

For the topping
100 g parmesan, grated
40 g butter

Preparation

Soak the mushrooms for 30 minutes in a bowl of lukewarm water. Chop the vegetables, meat and prosciutto into small pieces and gently sauté them for 20 to 30 minutes in the oil and butter. When the mixture starts to stick, add the wine. Allow the liquid to evaporate. Season with salt and pepper, add the mushrooms, chopped into small pieces, with their soaking water, the stock, the bouquet garni and the cloves. Cover and return to the heat for 40 minutes. Add the tomatoes halfway through the cooking. You should obtain a thick sauce.

To make the béchamel sauce melt the butter and sprinkle over the flour, while stirring. When the mixture colours, pour in the milk, stirring constantly to avoid lumps. Allow to thicken for 10 minutes, season with salt and add 1 pinch grated nutmeg. Allow the béchamel to cool; if it is too thick, add a little extra milk.

Cook the sheets of lasagne.

Butter a baking dish, spread a little béchamel on the bottom and alternate a layer of pasta, a layer of ragù and a little parmesan. Repeat the process three times, finishing with béchamel sauce. Top with grated parmesan and some pieces of butter. Bake in the oven for about 30 minutes. Allow to rest for 5 minutes before dividing into portions.

My suggestion

Serve lasagne as a one-dish meal with a green salad. Otherwise, make the portions small.

LASAGNE ARROTOLATO **ALLA ZUCCA**

Rolled pumpkin lasagne

For 8 people
Preparation time: 1 hour 30 minutes
Cooking time: 1 hour

For the filling
1,5 kg whole kent (jap) pumpkin
80 g crunchy amaretti biscuits
70 g Mostarda di Cremona
salt, white pepper
nutmeg, cinnamon
40g butter, melted
50 g parmesan cheese
1 whole egg + 1 egg yolk

400 g lasagne sheets
1 egg white

For the topping
50 g parmesan, grated
50 g butter

Preparation

Cut the pumpkin into quarters, remove the seeds and steam.

Crush the amaretti biscuits. Process the mostarda to make a purée. Mash the pumpkin, season with salt and white pepper, nutmeg and cinnamon. Add the butter, amaretti, mostarda, parmesan and egg. Taste to adjust the seasoning.

Cook the sheets of lasagne.

Lay out 3 or 4 sheets of lasagne: they should overlap lengthways. Brush the edges with the beaten egg white. Spread over a layer of filling, sprinkle with parmesan and roll up the sheets. Wrap in plastic wrap and chill for at least an hour in the fridge. Make another roll.

Butter a large baking dish. Cut the rolls into 3 cm slices and place them in the dish. Top with parmesan and pieces of butter and brown in the oven (180°C) for 20 minutes.

The authentic recipe

This is the tortelli alla zucca (with pumpkin), a specialty of Mantua and Emilia. It was my Aunt Edvige who gave me her recipe. Cook the pumpkin in the oven and dry in a frying pan to remove the moisture. Then make the tortelli (you only need a quarter of the amount of filling) and dress them with melted butter seasoned with sage and grated parmesan.

My suggestion

Make the rolls the day before or freeze them. Cut into small sections, they can be served warm with drinks.

Rotoli di spinaci *ricotta*

Rolled ricotta–spinach crêpes

For 6 people
Preparation time: 1 hour
Cooking time: 1 hour

For the filling

600 g fresh spinach
   or 300 g frozen spinach
80 g butter
1 garlic clove, halved
nutmeg
salt, pepper
250 g ricotta cheese
120 g mascarpone cheese
80 g parmesan cheese, grated
2 tablespoons breadcrumbs

250 ml milk
3 eggs
120 g plain (all-purpose) flour
20 g butter, melted
salt

To prepare the batter for the crêpes, place the flour in a large bowl. Add the eggs, milk, melted butter and salt and whisk until smooth. Cover with plastic film and allow to rest for 1 hour.

Steam the spinach then drain (or thaw frozen spinach). Heat a frying pan with 40 g of the butter and the garlic. Add the spinach, a good pinch of nutmeg, salt and pepper. Stir over a medium heat to 'dry' the spinach. Wait for it to cool to lukewarm before adding the ricotta, mascarpone and 50 g of the parmesan. Adjust the seasoning to taste.

Make the crêpes in a small non-stick frying pan, adding a little butter between each one. They must be quite thin and the first one doesn't count. Spread on each crêpe a little of the spinach filling and roll up tightly. Cut them across into four.

Butter a baking dish and arrange the small rolls in it. Sprinkle over the rest of the parmesan, breadcrumbs and a few pieces of butter. Brown in the oven for 10 minutes at 200°C.

Variations

For crêpes à la florentine, cover the rolls with a thin béchamel and a few spoonfuls of tomato passata (puréed tomatoes). You can also fold the crêpes in two and fill them with sautéed vegetables (asparagus, artichokes, mushrooms) mixed with just a little parmesan-flavoured béchamel sauce. Or cook them like sheets of lasagne.

ravioli

ravioli

//

Ravioli

Ravioli, tortellini, tortelloni, agnolotti, mezzelune, these are all names for stuffed pastas. The differences are in the size and shape. Ravioli are my favourite kind of pasta, the symbol of real family cooking: to make them successfully, you need a lot of patience and love. The best are home-made but I concede that you can enjoy delicious ravioli in very good restaurants.

Packaging

Try to buy fresh ravioli from Italian delicatessens. The 'three-cheese' varieties are rarely disappointing. Buy a few kinds of ravioli and only go back for the ones that seem perfect to you. The pre-packaged varieties you can buy often contain additives (breadcrumbs), the stuffing is processed by machine rather than hand-minced. Read the labels carefully.

Cooking

This is a delicate operation: half the time the pasta breaks open and the filling escapes into the pot. Cook ravioli in a fairly wide and shallow pot, in lightly salted simmering water, never at a high boil and no more than four servings at a time (about 500 g in total). Allow between 1 and 4 minutes depending on the thickness of the pasta (a little more if they have been frozen). Remove them from the water with a skimmer.

Dressing

Drain the ravioli and place them immediately in a dish kept warm on top of a saucepan of just-simmering water. Pour a little melted butter between each layer. For a small quantity (no more than three servings), toss them quickly in a hot frying pan in which you have melted 2 knobs of butter (10 g) per person with 2 or 3 tablespoons of cooking water. But don't stir them as you might break them. You can flavour the butter with sage leaves (4 leaves per person). Serve very hot with grated cheese.

When the filling is good, I don't use any cream or sauce, which tend to mask the taste of the ravioli.

Storing

Home-made ravioli or freshly prepared bought ravioli keep in the fridge (1 to 2 days maximum), protected with plastic film. To freeze, spread them out on a tray, keeping them quite separate, and leave them for a few hours in the freezer before packaging them in food bags. They keep frozen for 2 months. If the pasta is very thin, pre-cook them for 1 minute before freezing them.

AGNOLOTTI

//

For 6 people
Preparation time: 40 minutes
Cooking time: 3 minutes

For the filling

250 g spinach and/or silverbeet (Swiss chard)
30 g butter
250 g brasato
   (braised beef)
250 g bollito misto
   (beef pot-au-feu)
3 or 4 eggs
50 g parmesan cheese, grated
whole nutmeg
salt, pepper

850 g pasta dough
150 ml braised meat (brasato) juices
   and 60 g butter
30 g parmesan cheese, grated

Preparation

Soften the spinach in the butter. Chop finely with a knife along with the meat then add the eggs, parmesan, 1 pinch of nutmeg, salt and pepper. Rest the mixture for 1 hour in the fridge.

Roll out a very thin sheet of pasta (roll it out as you make the agnolotti so it doesn't dry out). Using a piping bag, pipe small mounds of filling at regular intervals. Roll out the rest of the dough into a sheet. Cover the first sheet. Press down the sheets of pasta so that they stick together. If the pasta has dried, brush with egg yolk mixed with a little water. Using a serrated pastry wheel, cut the agnolotti into 6 cm squares and cook them for about 3 minutes in a large pot of barely simmering water.

Blend the (hot) braising juices with the melted knob of butter, or else emulsify the 60 g of butter with a few tablespoons of water. Pour over dish to serve.

Tortelli **con pecorino**

For 6 people
Preparation time: 40 minutes
Cooking time: 3 minutes

For the filling

200 g mild pecorino cheese
120 g parmesan cheese
150 g ricotta cheese
1 egg
salt, pepper

850 g pasta dough
60 g butter
30 g parmesan cheese, grated

Preparation

Grate the pecorino and parmesan cheeses into a bowl, add the ricotta, then the egg. Season lightly with salt, and generously with pepper. Chill for 30 minutes.

Roll half of the pasta into a very thin sheet. Place small mounds of filling on the pasta at regular intervals then roll out the rest of the pasta to cover. Press down the sheets of pasta to make them stick together.

If the pasta has dried out a little, brush it with egg yolk mixed with a little water. Using a serrated pastry wheel, cut out the tortelli in 6 cm squares and cook them for about 3 minutes in a large saucepan of barely simmering water.

Melt the butter, add a few spoonfuls of cooking water and dress the well-drained tortelli. Sprinkle with parmesan.

My suggestion

I like to flavour the melted butter with the zest of an orange or add orange zest to the filling.

CASUNZIEI AMPEZZANI

Beetroot ravioli

For 6 people
Preparation time: 1 hour
Cooking time: 10 minutes

For the filling

600 g beetroot, cooked
100 g onions
50 g butter
1 potato, cooked
1 egg
salt, pepper

850 g pasta dough
80 g butter
⅓ cup poppyseeds
60 g parmesan or aged montasio cheese

Preparation

Peel the beetroot and purée them. Chop the onions and sauté them in 20 g of the butter for 5 to 6 minutes on a low heat, adding 2 tablespoons of water halfway through the cooking. Add the rest of the butter and allow it to melt before mixing in the puréed beetroot. Keep cooking on a gentle heat for 2 minutes, stirring, then allow to cool.

Mash the potato in a large bowl, mix in the egg and the cooled beetroot (the beetroot purée mustn't be too hot, or else it will cook the eggs). Season with salt and pepper.

Roll out half of the dough into a very thin sheet (roll it out as you make the casunziei so that it doesn't dry out). Place small mounds of filling on the pasta at regular intervals, then roll out the rest of the dough to cover this sheet. Press down all around to eliminate any air pockets and press the sheets of pasta together to make them stick. If the pasta has dried out a little, brush it with egg yolk mixed with a little water. Cut out the casunziei into half-moon shapes (between 6 and 8 cm in diameter) and cook them for about 3 minutes in a large saucepan of barely simmering water.

Melt the butter and add a few tablespoons of the casunziei cooking water. Dress the casunziei with this mixture and sprinkle them with poppy seeds. Serve with grated parmesan or aged montasio cheese.

Variation

These ravioli are a mountain region specialty (Veneto). I also enjoy them in a more rustic form (from Tyrol), filled simply with potato and onions, and dressed with butter and chives.

Tortelloni **con carciofi**

///

Artichoke tortelloni

For 6 people
Preparation time: 1 hour
Cooking time: 30 minutes

For the filling

8 small roman artichokes
1 lemon
2 tablespoons olive oil
1 garlic clove, chopped
2 marjoram sprigs
4 parsley sprigs
50 ml dry white wine
hot stock
salt, pepper
1 potato, cooked
1 egg yolk
40 g parmesan cheese, grated
whole nutmeg

850 g pasta dough
60 g butter
2 dozen sage leaves
60 g parmesan cheese, grated

Preparation

Prepare the dough two hours in advance to allow it to rest. Clean the artichokes: using a knife, remove 2 cm from the top and trim the stems, remove the toughest leaves. Cut the artichokes in two, remove the choke and soak them in water with a little lemon juice added.

Cut the artichokes again into eight and sauté them in a frying pan with the oil, garlic, marjoram and parsley. Moisten with the wine, allow to reduce, then add a little hot stock. When it has evaporated, add some more. Season with salt and pepper. Cover and allow to cook for 20 to 25 minutes: the artichokes should be very soft.

Chop them with a knife along with the potato and combine with the egg yolk, parmesan and 1 pinch of grated nutmeg.

Roll out half of the dough into a very thin sheet. Place small mounds of filling on the sheet at regular intervals then roll out the rest of the pasta to cover. Press down the sheets of pasta so that they stick together. Cut out the tortelloni into triangles using a serrated pastry wheel and fold over two of the points towards the middle. Cook them for 2 to 3 minutes in boiling salted water.

Melt the butter with the sage, moisten with a little of the pasta cooking water and pour over the pasta. Serve with the parmesan.

Storing

Use the tortelloni within 24 hours or freeze them, as artichokes have a tendency to oxidise.

Variations

To avoid the vegetables producing excess water, dry them in a frying pan and bind the sauce with a creamy cheese (ricotta, mascarpone, stracchino) or a hard one (parmesan), potato or eggs. Try this recipe with mushrooms, green asparagus, very finely diced zucchini or a mixture of greens (silverbeet (Swiss chard) and spinach).

dry pasta

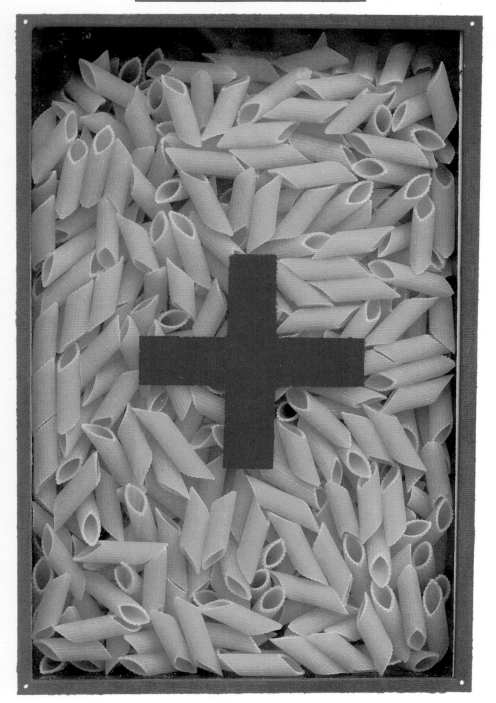

Salsa **di pomodoro** Tomato sauce

Tomato is a flagship ingredient in Italian cuisine, and yet it has only been used since the end of the eighteenth century …

Canned tomatoes

This is a basic pantry item, for Italians in any case: with a packet of spaghetti, some olive oil and a can of tomatoes (whole, crushed or as a sauce), you know you can always make a good meal!

Choose sauces made from 100% tomatoes or with a little salt and basil, but nothing more. Opt for products from the south of Italy. The most renowned come from San Marzano, in the Naples region, or from Pachino, in Sicily.

My home-made tomato sauce recipe

For 6 people, preparation time 30 minutes, cooking time 30 minutes. Finely chop 1 onion, 1 carrot and 1 celery stalk. In a large saucepan, sauté them gently for 10 minutes with 2 tablespoons olive oil. Peel 1.5 kg tomatoes, remove the seeds, chop the flesh roughly and add them to the saucepan. Allow to cook for 15 minutes, stirring from time to time. Add some salt and the leaves from a bunch of basil, torn with the hands. Pass through a food processor or food mill before adding the rest of the oil.

Variation

Replace the fresh tomatoes with 1.2 kg canned peeled tomatoes.

Fresh tomato sauce

Take advantage of summer to make a large quantity of sauce, with sun-drenched tomatoes (you can freeze it). Choose very ripe tomatoes.

If you cook the tomatoes with the skin on, put them through a food processor afterwards (unless the skin is very thin). If you prefer to peel them, make an incision in the base of the tomato and plunge into boiling water; take them out when the skin starts to crumple, let them cool a little, then peel. The skin should come off easily.

Packaging

• Peeled tomatoes (whole) in their juice. You crush them afterwards with a fork.
• Peeled and crushed tomato pulp is more practical. Ideal for making a chunky tomato sauce.
• Passata is made from peeled and seeded tomatoes which are then made into a purée (in a food processor or food mill). It is perfect for smooth sauces and very popular with children ...
• Tomato paste is often sold in a tube. A spoonful diluted in a little liquid is enough to flavour a sauce.

SALSE VELOCE

Quick pasta sauces

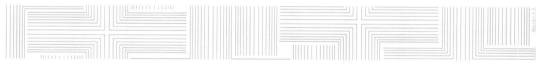

For 4 to 6 people
Preparation and cooking time: 20 minutes

Tomato sauce with garlic and basil

Heat 5 tablespoons of olive oil in a saucepan with 2 peeled garlic cloves (remove the sprout) and 6 hand-torn basil leaves. Add 1 kg of crushed tomato pulp, allow to cook for 2 minutes on a high heat then 15 minutes on a low heat. Stir occasionally. If the tomatoes are acidic, add 1 pinch of sugar at the beginning of the cooking. Season with salt. Finish the seasoning with a handful of basil leaves and 5 tablespoonfuls of olive oil, added without cooking.

Variations

Moisten the garlic and basil with 50 ml white wine before adding the tomatoes. Serve with fish or meat. For a milder flavour, replace the garlic with one large mild onion, finely chopped.

Amatriciana sauce

Sauté 1 large chopped onion, with 2 tablespoons of olive oil and 150 g finely diced pancetta. Add 1 kg crushed tomatoes and 1 small dried chilli. Season with salt. Allow to cook for 2 minutes on high heat, then 15 minutes on a medium heat, stirring frequently.

This is enough sauce for 500 g bucatini, cooked *al dente*. Add 2 tablespoons of olive oil to the pasta, pour over the sauce and sprinkle with pecorino or parmesan cheese. You can also use a mixture of the two cheeses.

Rocket, tomato and ricotta sauce

Make a tomato sauce with garlic. One minute before the end of cooking, add 150 g finely sliced rocket and mix in. Dress 500 g fusilli or penne with this sauce, serve in bowls and top with sheep's milk ricotta, grated pecorino and pepper.

Puttanesca sauce

Melt 6 anchovy fillets in 3 tablespoons of olive oil. Add 2 peeled garlic cloves, 1 tablespoonful of rinsed salted capers, roughly chopped. Stir over the heat, then add 1 kg crushed tomatoes, 1 small chopped chilli and 150 g pitted black olives sliced into rounds. Cook on a high heat for 2 minutes, then 15 minutes on medium heat, stirring frequently. Season with salt at the end of cooking and add 2 tablespoons of chopped flat-leaf (Italian) parsley. Dress 500 g spaghetti and sprinkle with parsley. No need for cheese, the anchovies are enough…

Variation

At the end of cooking, add well-drained chunks of tuna in oil.

Pasta *al forno*

Baked rigatoni with tomato and mozzarella

For 6 people
Preparation time: 30 minutes
Cooking time: 30 minutes

250 g mozzarella cheese
150 g smoked provola cheese
150 g parmesan cheese
250 g ricotta cheese
500 g rigatoni (large pasta tubes)
600 g tomato sauce
2 bunches of basil
4 to 6 tablespoons breadcrumbs
30 g butter
salt, pepper

Preparation

Chop the mozzarella and smoked provola cheeses into small pieces. Grate the parmesan and mix together with the ricotta.

Bring a large quantity of salted water to the boil to cook the rigatoni, reducing the cooking time indicated on the packet by 2 minutes.

Mix the pasta with the tomato sauce, half of the parmesan cheese and basil leaves.

Butter a baking dish, scatter a layer of breadcrumbs on the bottom, pour in half of the pasta, cover with half of the cheeses, season with salt and pepper and make another layer of pasta and another of cheese, season again with the rest of the basil (in leaves) slipped in between. Top with breadcrumbs and brown for about 20 minutes in the oven (180°C), with pieces of butter for a golden crust.

Variations

Every Italian has their own recipe for pasta al forno. My favourites: ragù, sausage, pecorino and mozzarella (typical of Apulia); béchamel sauce and finely sliced caciocavallo (Sicilian). A favourite for children: béchamel sauce, mozzarella, parmesan and finely diced prosciutto or ham.

Spaghettoni **alla carbonara e carciofi**

Spaghetti carbonara with artichokes

For 6 people
Preparation time: 30 minutes
Cooking time: 20 minutes

1 bunch small roman artichokes
1 lemon
100 ml olive oil
1 garlic clove, crushed
1 tablespoon chopped parsley
50 ml white wine (or stock)
salt, pepper
2 whole eggs + 4 egg yolks
150 g Pecorino Romano (or parmesan)
   cheese, grated
200 g guanciale (salt-cured pork cheek) or
   fatty pancetta
500 g spaghettoni (large spaghetti)

Preparation

Clean the artichokes: using a knife, remove 2 cm from the top and trim the stalks, remove the toughest leaves. Cut the artichokes in two, remove the choke and soak them in water with a little lemon juice added so that they don't discolour. Cut the artichokes again into eight, then cook them over medium heat in a frying pan, with 2 tablespoons of the oil, the garlic, parsley, white wine, salt and pepper. They should stay firm to the bite.

In a large bowl, emulsify the eggs with the grated cheese, salt, pepper and 1 tablespoon of the oil. Cut the guanciale or pancetta into thin strips. Brown in the frying pan with a little olive oil.

Cook the pasta until al dente in a large quantity of boiling salted water. Add a few tablespoons of the pasta cooking water to the beaten eggs (to prevent the eggs from cooking when you mix them through the pasta).

Add the well-drained pasta to a hot frying pan with a few tablespoons of its cooking water, the rest of the oil and the guanciale. Sauté quickly then combine in a large bowl with the beaten eggs and grated cheese. The sauce will form a runny cream. Serve topped with the sautéed artichokes.

The authentic recipe

I have added sautéed artichokes to a classic spaghetti carbonara, which is made the same way as the authentic Roman recipe, with guanciale or pancetta, and with no cream.

SPAGHETTI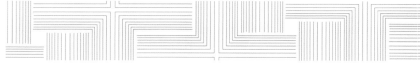
ALLE VONGOLE

Spaghetti with clams

For 6 people
Preparation time: 40 minutes
Cooking time: 30 minutes

1 kg clams (vongole)
100 ml olive oil
2 or 3 garlic cloves
600 g fresh tomatoes, for sauce
salt, pepper
500 g spaghetti
1 bunch of parsley, chopped

Preparation

Carefully wash the clams in running water. Place them in a large frying pan with 100 ml of water and a drizzle of olive oil. Allow to bubble until the clams open: remove the open clams using a skimmer and place them in a strainer. Allow them to cool. Discard any clams that do not open.

Filter the cooking water through a very fine strainer (you can line it with muslin (cheesecloth) so that no sand gets through).

Rinse out the frying pan. Pour in half of the oil and heat it a little before adding the garlic cloves (that you can remove at the end of cooking), the tomato sauce, 1 pinch of salt and the cooking water from the clams. Allow to cook gently until the sauce starts to thicken.

Meanwhile, bring some water to the boil in a large saucepan, add salt and cook the spaghetti until *al dente*.

Set aside a quarter of the clams in their shells for decoration, shell the rest (discard the shells). Just before dressing the pasta, add the shelled clams to the sauce with three-quarters of the chopped parsley. Drain the spaghetti and sauté it in the sauce with the remaining olive oil and a few tablespoonfuls of its cooking water. Serve very hot with some pepper, the rest of the chopped parsley and the clams in their shell to garnish.

Variations

This dish is also excellent without tomatoes, just with the slightly reduced juice from the clams, flavoured with garlic, olive oil, parsley and chilli (to taste). You can replace the clams (or some of them) with mussels and/or cockles.

Paccheri **al pesce spada, melanzane e rosmarino**

Swordfish, eggplant and rosemary pasta

For 6 people
Preparation time: 30 minutes
Cooking time: 20 minutes

100 ml olive oil
3 sprigs rosemary, leaves chopped
2 garlic cloves
2 large eggplants (aubergines)
500 g paccheri (or short pasta)
300 g fresh swordfish in 2 cm steaks
salt, pepper

Preparation

In a small saucepan, gently heat half of the olive oil, the chopped rosemary leaves, and 1 halved garlic clove (to be removed before serving), for 2 minutes. Set aside.

Dice the eggplant. Cook it in several batches (to avoid overcrowding) in a non-stick frying pan with 1 tablespoon of olive oil, 1 garlic clove (removed at the end of cooking) and some salt. When the eggplant is soft and golden, remove from the frying pan and keep warm.

Cook the paccheri until al dente in a large quantity of boiling salted water (larger pasta requires more water). Stir them gently, especially during the first 5 minutes of cooking.

Meanwhile, cut the swordfish into cubes of about 2 cm and pan-fry them for 1 minute on a high heat with 2 tablespoons olive oil. Season with salt and pepper. Set aside.

Drain the pasta and sauté it in the frying pan with the rosemary oil, a few spoonfuls of its cooking water and the eggplant. Serve on a large dish topped with the swordfish.

Variation

Take advantage of the summer months to enjoy Mediterranean swordfish. You can also use tuna for this recipe, accompanied by tomatoes marinated in garlic and olive oil and a combination of herbs (basil, thyme and oregano).

Pasta **alle bietole**

Pasta with silverbeet

For 6 people
Preparation time: 40 minutes
Cooking time: 30 minutes

1 kg fresh broad (fava) beans (300 to 400 g
    podded)
1 large bunch silverbeet (Swiss chard) (800 g
    to 1 kg)
1 bunch bulb spring onions (scallions)
    (or one very large onion)
100 ml olive oil
salt, pepper
chilli powder
200 g blanched almonds
500 g mezze millerighe
    (or short pasta)
200 g Pecorino Romano (or ricotta salata or
    parmesan) cheese, grated

Preparation

To peel the broad beans, first boil them for 30 seconds and refresh them under running water. Remove the skin. Wash the silverbeet, separate the stalks from the leaves and steam them separately: they should be just tender.

In a large saucepan, gently brown the onions, thinly sliced, in 3 tablespoons of olive oil. Add the peeled broad beans and a glass of water (or stock). Season with salt and pepper. Cover and allow to cook until the broad beans are tender (between 5 and 15 minutes depending on the type of broad bean).

Mix in the silverbeet, chopped into small pieces, and 'dry' the mixture over a gentle heat. Season with salt and add some chilli powder.

Toast the almonds in a dry frying pan and chop them.

Bring a large saucepan of water to the boil, add salt and cook the mezze millerighe until al dente. Drain it and toss for 1 minute on a medium heat in the saucepan with the vegetables, the remaining olive oil and a few tablespoonfuls of the cooking water.

Off the heat, add half of the almonds and some of the grated cheese. Mix well. Serve hot, sprinkled with the rest of the almonds and cheese.

The authentic recipe

This dish is cooked in Apulia using Catalonian witlof (chicory/ Belgian endive), very closely related to wild chicory. Use this instead of silverbeet if you manage to find some. It is superb.

My suggestion

As it is, this is a completely vegetarian recipe. But you can embellish it with some rolled pancetta (150 g diced, browned along with the broad beans) or diced bacon.

Spaghetti *ai riccio di mare*

Spaghettini with sea urchin

For 6 people
Preparation time: 20 minutes
Cooking time: 10 minutes

30+ sea urchins or canned sea urchin meat
500 g spaghettini
200 ml olive oil
2 garlic cloves
½ bunch parsley, chopped
salt, pepper

Preparation

Cut open the sea urchins using scissors, halfway up, and remove the meat with a small spoon. Set it aside in a large bowl with the liquid from inside the sea urchins.

Bring a large saucepan of water to the boil, add salt and cook the spaghettini until al dente.

In a wide frying pan, heat the olive oil for 1 minute with the garlic cloves (which are then immediately removed). Off the heat, add three-quarters of the parsley and the sea urchin meat.

Drain the pasta and toss it quickly in the frying pan with the urchins. Serve hot, sprinkled with the rest of the parsley and seasoned with pepper.

Sea urchins the way I like them

This is a memory from my holidays by the sea in Sicily. We used to dive under the water to pick them from the rocks, and we opened and ate them there on the spot...

My practical tips

Learn how to choose sea urchins, which should be brightly coloured, heavy in the hand, and with their spines whole. Eat them the same day or keep them for no more than 48 hours in the fridge, wrapped in a damp cloth. Female sea urchin meat is orange to bright red, much better than that of male sea urchins (yellow). But you need to open them to check the colour to determine whether they're male or female.

Rita from Da Rita

Il Tre

ORECCHIETTE PICCANTI CON BROCCOLI

Orecchiette with chilli and broccoli

For 6 people
Preparation time: 15 minutes
Cooking time: 15 minutes

100 ml olive oil
2 garlic cloves
1 dried chilli (according to your taste)
3 anchovy fillets, rinsed (or anchovy paste)
1.5 kg broccoli
500 g traditionally made orecchiette (or short pasta)
100 g Pecorino Romano or parmesan cheese
salt, freshly ground black pepper

Preparation

Heat half the oil in a frying pan, add the garlic cloves (remove them at the end of cooking), the dried chilli and melt in the anchovies. Set aside.

Wash the broccoli and separate into small florets. Cook them in boiling salted water (keep the water for the pasta) then remove them with a skimmer so you don't crush them and sauté them quickly in the frying pan with the chilli-flavoured oil. Taste before seasoning with salt and pepper.

Cook the pasta in the broccoli cooking water (add more water if necessary), then drain it well. Toss it in the frying pan with the broccoli, the rest of the oil, a few tablespoonfuls of its cooking water and half the cheese, grated. Serve very hot with the rest of the cheese, shaved on top.

The authentic recipe

This is a specialty of Apulia which is made with rapini (cime di rapa) instead of broccoli. This is the young growth of a plant related to the turnip, which I have managed to find in Portuguese stores.

PESTO
DI BASILICO

Basil pesto

For 6 people
Preparation time: 15 minutes

20 g pine nuts
4 bunches of basil
10 g walnut kernels
1 garlic clove
sea salt, pepper
100 ml olive oil
30 g parmesan cheese, grated

Preparation

Toast the pine nuts in a non-stick frying pan, stirring constantly.

Clean the basil leaves with a damp cloth and place them in the bowl of a food processor with the toasted pine nuts, walnuts, garlic, salt and pepper. Process quickly. At the last moment, add the parmesan and the oil, in a thin stream.

My suggestion

Place the bowl of the food processor and its blade in the freezer for 1 hour. This avoids the sauce overheating and losing its aromas.

Uses

With this amount of pesto, you can dress 500 g pasta. So that it blends more easily, add 4 tablespoons of the pasta cooking water and a drizzle of olive oil.

In Genoa, they add to the boiling water (before the pasta) 150 g green beans and 200 g diced potato, the pasta (linguine) is added when it comes back to the boil, afterwards it is dressed with the pesto.

Mix this pesto with ricotta and spread on bread or add it to a filling for a tart or lasagne.

Make a pesto without parmesan cheese to flavour fish, meat or vegetables.

Pesto « **alla Siciliana** »

Sicilian-style pesto

For 6 to 8 people
Preparation time: 10 minutes

40 g black olives, pitted
40 g green olives, pitted
40 g salted capers
40 g sundried tomatoes
1 tablespoon oregano
1 tablespoon rosemary, chopped
2 tablespoons parsley, chopped
100 ml olive oil

Preparation

Process all of the ingredients together until you have a smooth mixture. Don't rinse the capers completely, this will save you from having to add salt.

Uses

Blend the pesto with a little cooking water and use it to dress hot pasta, a pasta salad or rice.

Spread on some bread or use it to stuff tomatoes, capsicums (peppers).

These pestos keep for a few days in the fridge. Put them in a glass jar, cover with olive oil and close the lid tightly.

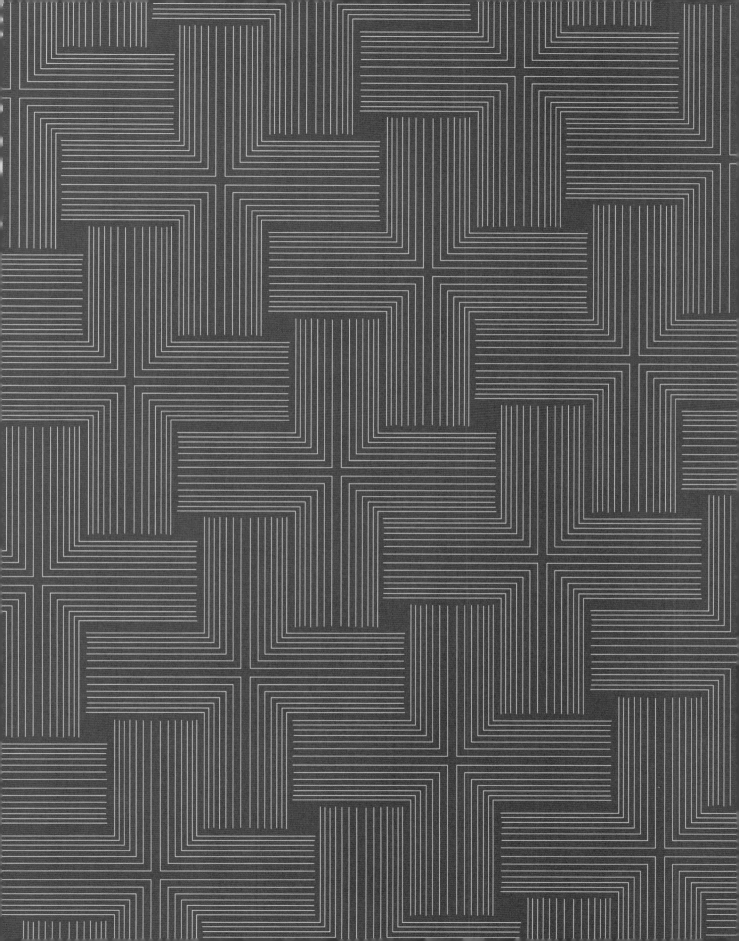

Conchiglioni con pesto di rucola
e verdura al dente

Conchiglioni with rocket pesto and vegetables

For 6 people
Preparation time: 30 minutes
Cooking time: 30 minutes

2 eggplants (aubergines)
3 medium-sized zucchini (courgettes)
3 capsicums (peppers) of different colours
50 to 60 ml olive oil
3 garlic cloves
salt
500 g conchiglioni
   (or large pasta, or short pasta)
6 tablespoons rocket pesto
100 g ricotta salata (optional), grated

Preparation

Wash all the vegetables and then finely dice. Sauté each separately in a non-stick frying pan with 1 tablespoon of olive oil for each batch, 1 garlic clove (removed after cooking) for each batch and salt, stirring frequently. The zucchini and capsicum should be still firm, the eggplant soft. Combine all of the vegetables in the frying pan.

Meanwhile, cook the pasta shapes until al dente in a large quantity of boiling salted water (stir them often during the first 5 minutes of cooking). Drain and dress them with the rest of the olive oil and the pesto diluted with a few tablespoonfuls of cooking water. Add the vegetables last and mix together. Serve hot, or cold as a salad, with the ricotta salata (if using).

My suggestion

This is one of my favourite dishes in the summer months: pan-fried vegetables, still al dente, with a pesto that coats and flavours the pasta wonderfully. I like to serve it cold for a picnic. You can try different vegetables, depending on what's available and your own preferences. Pair baby zucchini with a basil and mint pesto for example, or eggplants and marinated tomatoes with a basil pesto.

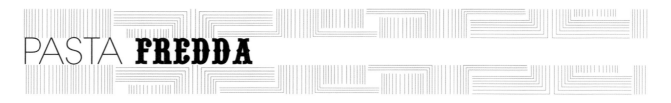

PASTA **FREDDA**

Pasta salads

Pasta fredda is the Italian name for a pasta salad. A simple, balanced and ultra-practical dish, perfect for a picnic, a large buffet or the lunch break. It can be made in advance (at least 1 hour but no more than 8 hours).

You can serve it as a starter (allow 50 g dry pasta per person) or as a main course (80–90 g per person). Use durum wheat pasta (without eggs), it stays firmer! And choose a short pasta, which holds the sauce better.

Cook the pasta until very al dente, drain and rinse under running water for 2 to 3 seconds. Drain it again then mix in some oil straight away so it doesn't stick together. Depending on the other ingredients, you can mix these into the lukewarm pasta or let it cool on a tray. And always eat the salad at room temperature.

Express flavours

To give flavour to your salad, it is important to coat the pasta with a tasty dressing: olive paste or pesto (basil, rocket, pistachio or Sicilian-style), diluted with a little of the pasta cooking water. Then add the other ingredients.

My favourites

• Marinated tomatoes, basil pesto and mozzarella cheese.

• Canned tuna, sun-dried tomatoes, salted capers and dried oregano.

• Bottarga, rocket and olive oil.

• Caponata.

• Roasted stuffed tomatoes.

• Pistachio pesto, prosciutto, toasted pine nuts.

Pasticcio di piccioni

Pasta with pigeon in pastry

For 6 people
Preparation time: 1 hour
Cooking time: 1 hour 30 minutes

For the shortcrust pastry

400 g plain (all-purpose) flour
pinch of salt
200 g butter
50 g sugar
3 egg yolks

For the pigeon ragù

150 g onion
100 g carrot
100 g celery
2 tablespoons olive oil
40 g butter
100 g prosciutto slices
2 pigeons, cleaned, halved, skin removed
100 ml dry marsala
4 pigeon livers, quartered
salt, pepper
300 to 400 ml vegetable stock
200 g boneless, skinless chicken breast
200 g peas, podded

For the béchamel sauce

40 g butter
40 g plain (all-purpose) flour
800 ml milk
salt
1 nutmeg, grated

400 g reginette (wide durum wheat tagliatelle
   with serrated edges)
70 g parmesan cheese, grated

Preparation

First make the shortcrust pastry. Mound the flour on the work surface, add 1 pinch of salt and the butter in small pieces (at room temperature). Work in with the fingertips for a crumbly consistency. Incorporate the sugar, egg yolks and a few tablespoons of water. Shape into a ball and chill in the fridge for at least 30 minutes.

Heat half the oil and 20 g butter in a large deep frying pan over a medium low heat. Add the onion, carrot, celery and prosciutto, saute for 6–7 minutes or until light golden. Increase heat, add pigeons and brown for 2–3 minutes. Add marsala, simmer until reduced. Reduce heat to low and add 125 ml stock, cover and simmer for 30 minutes, adding a little more stock if necessary.

Bone the pigeons and chop the meat into small pieces. Combine with the chicken. Cook the peas in boiling salted water, then add them to the ragù.

For the béchamel sauce, melt the butter in a saucepan, add the flour and mix well. When it begins to colour, pour in the milk little by little, stirring constantly. Allow to thicken over a medium heat for 10 minutes after coming to the boil. Season with salt and grated nutmeg. Allow the sauce to cool a little, adding a little stock if it is too thick.

Put the reginette on to cook in a large saucepan of boiling salted water, then drain them halfway through cooking. Dress with the béchamel sauce, ragù and parmesan.

Knead the dough for 30 seconds and make two rounds of pastry, a large one for the base of the dish and a smaller one to cover. Line a round (24 cm) dish with baking paper, lay in the larger pastry round and pour in the pasta. Pack down with the ragù and cover with the other round. Brush with beaten egg mixed with 1 tablespoon of milk and prick the pastry with a fork. Bake in the oven for about 25 minutes (180°C). Wait for 5 minutes before serving.

TIMBALLO **NAPOLETANA**

Timbale of macaroni and chicken liver ragù

For 6 people
Preparation time: 30 minutes
Cooking time: 1 hour
30 minutes

25 g dried porcini mushrooms or 200 g fresh
    porcini mushrooms
50 g French shallots, finely chopped
3 tablespoons olive oil
40 g butter
1 fresh or canned black truffle (optional)
350 g chicken livers
salt, pepper
200 g breadcrumbs
1 egg
400 g fresh tomatoes, peeled and crushed
    (or canned crushed tomatoes)
400 g ziti or rigatoni (tubular pasta)

Preparation

Soak the dried mushrooms in a bowl of lukewarm water for 20 minutes, then squeeze them dry and chop them roughly.

In a frying pan, gently cook the French shallots and the mushroom for 6 to 8 minutes with 1 tablespoon of the oil and 10 g of the butter (add a little water if necessary). Then add 20 g of the butter, the truffle, in shavings, and the chicken livers, cleaned and cut into two or three. Sauté for 1 or 2 minutes, season with salt and pepper.

Add the tomatoes and continue to cook for a further 5 minutes (the sauce should be quite liquid). Taste to adjust the seasoning if it is necessary.

Butter a charlotte mould (1.5 litre capacity), coat the inside with half the breadcrumbs, pour in the beaten egg and tip the mould in all directions to coat with the egg and coat again with the remaining breadcrumbs. Tap off the excess.

Put the pasta on to cook in a large saucepan of boiling salted water and drain it almost halfway through the cooking (very al dente). Dress with the liquid from the sauce and 2 tablespoons of oil.

Pour half of the pasta into the mould, cover with the chicken liver ragù and finish with the remaining pasta. Press down lightly and cover with buttered baking paper.

Bake in the oven (160°C) for 45 to 60 minutes. Allow to rest for 5 minutes before unmoulding onto a large plate. Serve hot.

Variation

I also enjoy this timbale with a meat ragù (veal, duck or lamb bolognese sauce) with peas or artichokes.

gnocchi

Gnocchi *di patate*

Potato gnocchi

For 6 people
Preparation time: 30 minutes
Cooking time: 3 minutes

1 kg potatoes
250 g plain (all-purpose) flour
1 egg
salt, nutmeg

Preparation

Wash the potatoes and cook them for about 40 minutes in boiling salted water. Remove the skin and mash them directly on floured work surface. Cool until lukewarm.

Flour your hands. Make a mound of the mashed potato with a hollow in the centre and pour into the middle three-quarters of the flour, the egg, the salt and a good pinch of nutmeg. Then mix in the rest of the flour very quickly until you have a smooth and pliable mixture.

Take a little of the dough and make a 1.5 cm-thick roll, working with floured hands. Repeat several times. Cut the rolls into 2.5 cm sections and place these on a lightly floured tea towel.

Bring a large quantity of water to the boil in a large saucepan and add salt. Add the gnocchi. As soon as they rise to the surface, remove them straight away using a skimmer. Add sauce without delay.

Sauces

Classic: melted butter (between 60 and 100 g) seasoned with sage, and some grated parmesan (60 g) sprinkled over.
Venetian-style: replace the sage with 1 large pinch of ground cinnamon.
With tomato sauce: make a tomato sauce, replacing the oil at the end with a large knob of butter.
With ragù: dress the gnocchi with a bolognese sauce.
With Gorgonzola.

My suggestions

Don't make the gnocchi too far ahead of serving time, or they will become gluey and quite soft ... If you have made a very large quantity, cook them and keep the excess in an oiled dish; you can then reheat them in the boiling water (but don't keep them more than 24 hours). You can make an eggless dough, adding in this case 200 g flour.

Gnocchi **di ricotta e spinaci**

Ricotta and spinach gnocchi

For 6 people
Preparation time: 40 minutes
Cooking time: 20 minutes

70 g French shallots
150 g butter
12 sage leaves
5 small marjoram sprigs
   or 1 bunch basil
250 g cooked spinach
1 large egg
500 g ricotta cheese
100 g parmesan cheese, grated
salt, pepper
nutmeg
150 g plain (all-purpose) flour

Preparation

Chop the shallots and sauté them gently with 2 knobs of the butter and the chopped herbs. Moisten with a little water and add some more when it evaporates.

Process the spinach with the egg and half the shallots. Place them in a bowl, add the ricotta, 60 g of the parmesan cheese, salt, pepper and nutmeg. Combine well before adding the flour in several stages.

To test the dough, form some mixture into a quenelle and drop it into lightly salted boiling water for 2 minutes. If it is too soft, add a little flour to the dough. Cook the gnocchi in several batches in boiling water, remove them using a skimmer and place them on a large oiled dish. Drop them back in the boiling water for 30 seconds before serving them dressed with melted butter and the rest of the shallots. Sprinkle over the remaining parmesan.

My suggestions

Prepare the gnocchi the day before and keep them in the fridge, covered with plastic wrap. For the sauce, you can use less butter and add a few spoonfuls of the gnocchi's cooking water. Or serve with a tomato sauce with butter and basil.

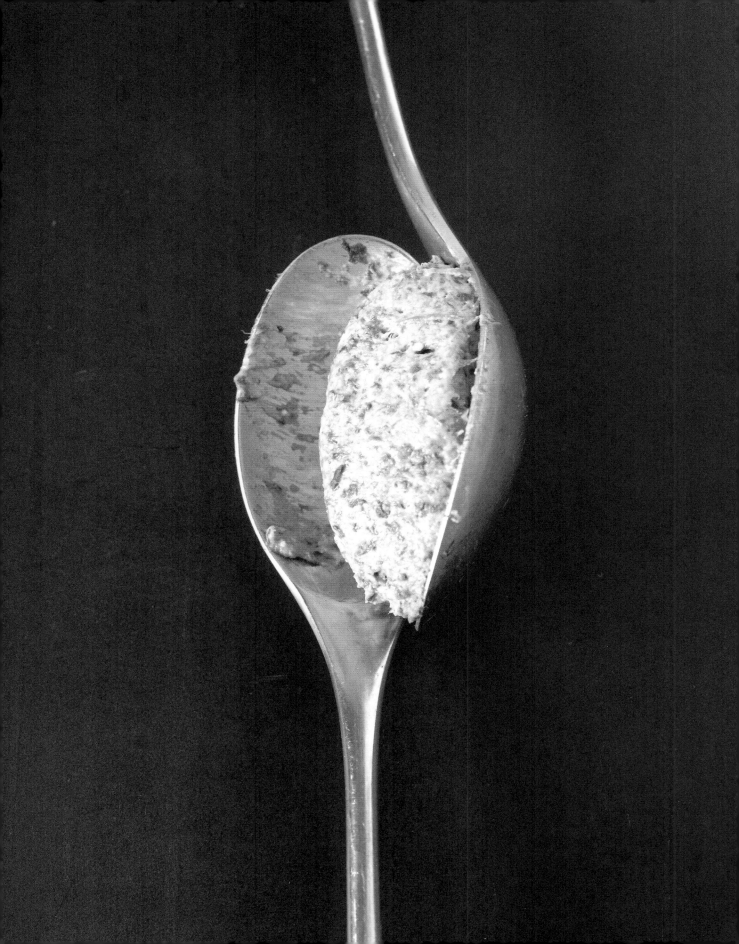

GNOCCHI DI ZUCCA

Pumpkin gnocchi

For 8 people
Preparation and cooking time:
1 hour

2 kg pumpkin (winter squash)
250 g ricotta cheese
50 g parmesan cheese, grated
160 to 190 g plain (all-purpose) flour
2 eggs
salt, pepper
nutmeg

80 g butter, melted
20 sage leaves
80 g parmesan cheese, grated
 or 200 g smoked ricotta cheese

Preparation

Cut the pumpkin into pieces, remove the seeds, and cook it in the oven (160°C) for 1 hour, under a sheet of foil. Prick a piece with a fork to check whether it is cooked through: it should be very soft.

Purée the pumpkin using a food processor or food mill, then mix in the ricotta, parmesan, flour (sifted several times), the yolks of the eggs, salt, pepper and nutmeg. Add the egg whites, whipped to soft peaks, and a little extra parmesan if the mixture is too soft.

Make the mixture into quenelles using two tablespoons. Drop them in a large saucepan of lightly salted boiling water. Allow about 3 minutes cooking time and remove the gnocchi using a skimmer. Place them in a dish. Pour over the butter seasoned with sage leaves and sprinkle with parmesan or smoked ricotta.

My suggestions

Make the gnocchi in advance and reheat them for 30 seconds in boiling water or in the oven to brown them on top. In autumn, serve with mixed sautéed mushrooms.

Variation

Try this more rustic version: mix 500 g mashed pumpkin with 2 egg yolks, 100 g plain (all-purpose) flour, salt and pepper. Make the gnocchi and drop them into boiling water. Dress with sage-flavoured butter and parmesan cheese.

GNOCCHI DI SEMOLINO **ALLA ROMANA**

Roman-style gnocchi

For 6 people
Preparation time: 30 minutes
Cooking time: 30 minutes

1 litre milk
250 g fine semolina
140 g butter
salt
80 g parmesan cheese, grated
2 egg yolks

Preparation

Heat the milk in a saucepan. When it starts to boil, pour in the semolina, stirring with a whisk. Add 20 g of the butter and the salt. Keep the saucepan on the heat for 20 minutes, constantly whisking briskly.

Off the heat, add 50 g of the butter and 50 g of the parmesan cheese. Allow to cool to lukewarm before mixing in the egg yolks.

Tip the semolina out onto a sheet of damp baking paper and try to spread it out evenly to a thickness of 1 cm, using a spatula or knife blade dipped in hot water. Allow to cool completely.

Using a glass or a cookie cutter, cut out rounds 5 to 6 cm in diameter. Place the gnocchi in a large buttered dish; they should overlap slightly. Cover with the rest of the parmesan and melt and pour over butter. Brown in the oven for the remaining 15 minutes.

My suggestion

This is a light, appealing dish that children love. I like to serve it with a tomato sauce.

canederli

Bread gnocchi

For 6 people
Preparation time: 45 minutes
Cooking time: 30 minutes

400 g stale white sandwich bread
250 ml milk, lukewarm
2 bulb spring onions, sliced
60 g butter
1 tablespoon chopped parsley
5 eggs
salt, nutmeg
200 g smoked pancetta
1 bunch chives, snipped

Preparation

Cut the bread into small cubes and mix with the milk. Allow to soak for a few minutes.

In a frying pan soften the onions over a gentle heat in 30 g of butter.

Mix the onions with the bread, parsley, eggs, salt and a good pinch of nutmeg. If the dough is too soft, add some flour. If it is too stiff, moisten with a little milk.

Use your hands to shape balls, 5 cm in diameter, and cook them in boiling salted water for 15 minutes.

Dice the pancetta and brown it in the remaining butter. Place the drained gnocchi on a plate, scatter over the pancetta and dress with the melted butter from the pancetta pan and the chives.

My suggestion

This dish is typical of the Alto-Adige region. You can dress it with just the melted butter and chives. Serve these gnocchi with a sauté of veal or beef.

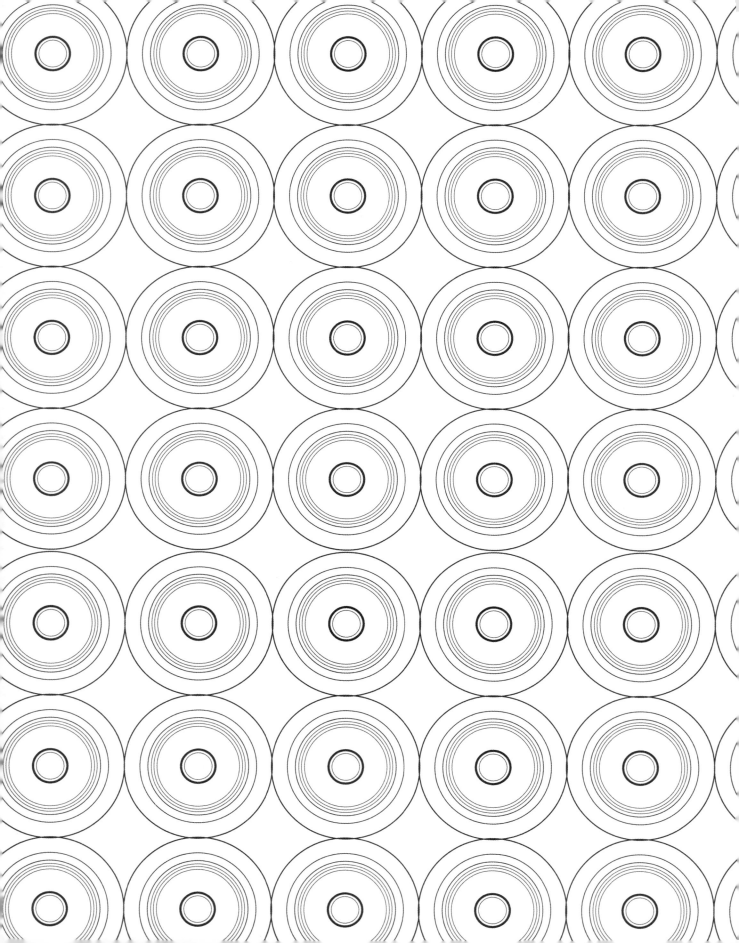

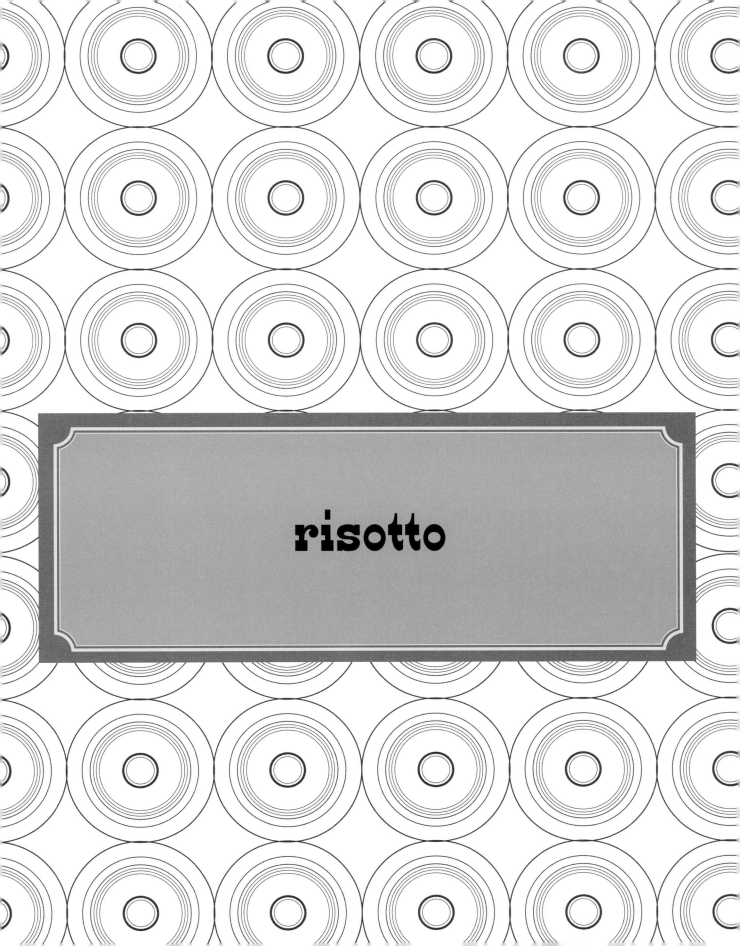

risotto

Risotto

The ingredients for a successful risotto

Italian rice of the *carnaroli* (the Rolls-Royce), *vialone nano* or *arborio* varieties. These short-grain rices are high in starch, absorb liquid well and stay firm to the bite. Allow about 70 g per person.

Meat or vegetable stock. Preferably home-made. Otherwise, buy some organic stock (without added flavour enhancers), in cube or powder form. Allow 3 times the quantity of stock for 1 volume of rice. Wine is optional.

Finely chopped French shallots or onions, butter and parmesan cheese. Allow 10 g of each ingredient per person.

One or several ingredients to flavour the risotto: vegetables, cheese, meat or fish, the choice is very wide …

The tools

Use a large, deep frying pan with a thick base and a lid, a wooden spoon, another saucepan for the stock, a ladle to pour it in and a cheese grater.

Express risotto

If you are in a hurry, sauté the rice in the oil or butter with the onion, pour in all of the stock at once and allow the rice to cook for 15 minutes on a very low heat, covered and without mixing. The result is not bad, but nevertheless not the same as true risotto.

Vary the recipe according to the season

In spring, risotto primavera, with green asparagus, peas and roman artichokes, or risotto with strawberries, scampi and ginger.

In summer, risotto with capsicum, fresh tomatoes and basil, with zucchini and mullet fillets, with melon and lemon, with cuttlefish ink, with seafood.

In autumn, risotto with wild mushrooms, with white truffle paste, with Hokkaido pumpkin, with beetroot, with scallops and saffron, with smoked *scamorza* (cheese), rocket and fresh walnuts, with chicken livers and red onions.

In winter, risotto with radicchio di Treviso (a late-season radicchio), with leeks and fresh sausage, with kale and speck (smoked ham), with Mont-d'Or cheese and toasted hazelnuts, with saffron Milanese-style, with Gorgonzola, mascarpone and pears, with potatoes, pancetta and rosemary.

Risotto *con porcini e zafferano*

Risotto with porcini and saffron

For 6 people
Preparation time: 15 minutes
Cooking time: 25 minutes

2 pinches saffron threads
1.5 litres chicken stock
50 g dried porcini mushrooms
2 tablespoons olive oil
80 g butter
80 g French shallots
400 g carnaroli rice
100 ml dry white wine
salt, pepper
60 g parmesan cheese, grated

Preparation

Infuse the saffron in 200 ml of the hot stock. Soak the mushrooms for at least 30 minutes in lukewarm water (change the water once). Chop them roughly, strain the soaking water and add it to the saffron stock.

In a saucepan, heat the oil with 20 g of the butter and sauté the chopped shallots over a gentle heat. After 3 minutes, add the mushrooms. Stir for 30 seconds and pour in the rice. Continue to stir for 2 minutes on a high heat then moisten with the wine. Allow it to evaporate before adding the hot stock, ladleful by ladleful, until it is almost absorbed. When the risotto is almost cooked, add the saffron with the stock.

Adjust the seasoning before incorporating the rest of the butter and the parmesan, off the heat. Cover and wait 2 minutes before serving.

My suggestion

Always have dried porcini mushrooms and saffron on hand so you can prepare this risotto whenever you have unexpected guests. In autumn, you can adapt the recipe by using fresh porcini mushrooms (allow 100 g per person).

Express variations

For a 'deluxe' version, flavour a plain risotto with white truffle paste. To add a surprising touch to this risotto, colour it with a jar of cuttlefish ink sauce.

RISOTTO CON TALEGGIO E PERE

Risotto with taleggio and pears

For 6 people
Preparation time: 20 minutes
Cooking time: 30 minutes

3 pears
80 g butter
350 g taleggio cheese
1 onion, finely chopped
2 tablespoons olive oil
450 g carnaroli or arborio rice
100 ml dry white wine
salt
1.5 litres chicken stock
   or vegetable stock
pepper
60 g parmesan cheese, grated

Preparation

Cut one of the pears into 18 very thin slices (for decoration) and pan-fry them for 1 minute on each side in 20 g of the butter. Peel the remaining pears and chop them into small dice. Chop the taleggio into small pieces (remove the rind).

Soften the onion in the olive oil on a gentle heat. After 5 minutes, add the rice and sauté on a high heat, until it looks pearly (2 minutes). Moisten with the wine and allow to evaporate, stirring. Season with salt.

Pour in a ladle of very hot stock and continue to cook on a medium heat, stirring frequently. When the stock is absorbed, moisten with another ladleful, and so on …

As soon as the risotto is cooked, add the taleggio and the diced pears, season with pepper and combine well. Off the heat, mix in the rest of the butter and the parmesan, cover and allow to rest for 2 minutes. Serve with the sautéed pears.

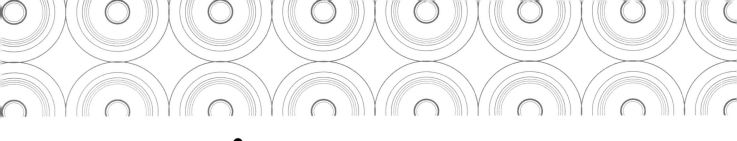

venere rice

This is a black wholegrain rice that has been cultivated in China for centuries and today is grown in the Po valley. It is high in fibre, firm and aromatic.

You can cook it in salted water (18 minutes for pre-cooked rice, otherwise 40 minutes) and sauté it in a frying pan with the flavouring of your choice. Ideal with prawns, scampi, al dente vegetables or for serving with meat or fish.

RISOTTO
PRIMAVERA

This is a spring dish that you can make with your favourite seasonal vegetables.

For 6 people
Preparation time: 30 minutes
Cooking time: 30 minutes

1 onion
salt, pepper

3 small roman artichokes
250 g zucchini (courgette)
1 bunch green asparagus (350 g)
6 tablespoons olive oil
salt, pepper
60 g butter, cold
1 onion, chopped
400 g vialone nano rice
100 ml dry white wine
1.5 litres vegetable stock
2 small new carrots
250 g peas, podded
5 parsley sprigs, chopped
60 g parmesan cheese, grated

Preparation

Cut the artichokes into eight, the zucchini into small dice and the asparagus in rounds (reserve the tips and discard the bottom 3 cm of the base). Pan-fry the vegetables separately, using 4 tablespoons of the olive oil, for 2 or 3 minutes for each. Season with salt and pepper. Blanch the asparagus tips for 2 minutes.

In a large, deep frying pan, heat the remaining olive oil and 20 g of the butter, add the onion and allow to cook gently for 5 minutes. Pour in the rice. Stir with a wooden spoon over a high heat until it becomes translucent (allow 1 or 2 minutes).

Moisten with the wine, evaporate, then season with salt. Pour in a ladleful of very hot stock, add the carrots chopped into small dice and the peas. As soon as the stock is absorbed, add another ladleful and continue doing this until all the stock has been used. Three minutes before the end of cooking, add all of the other vegetables to the pan.

Remove the pan from the heat and adjust the seasoning. Add the chopped parsley, remaining butter and parmesan. Stir in quickly. Cover and allow to rest for 2 minutes. Serve *all'onda*, which is to say, still fluid.

RISOTTO **ALLA SBIRRAGLIA**

Risotto with chicken and vegetables

For 6 people
Preparation time: 30 minutes
Cooking time: 40 minutes

4 chicken thighs
1.5 litres vegetable stock
2 tablespoons olive oil
80 g butter
2 medium-sized onions, finely chopped
2 medium-sized carrots, finely chopped
2 celery stalks, finely chopped
400 g vialone nano rice
150 ml dry white wine
sage leaves
salt
60 g parmesan cheese, grated

Preparation

Remove the skin from the chicken thighs and poach them for 15 minutes in the stock. Allow them to cool. Remove the flesh from the bones and break up into small pieces. Set aside.

In a wide, deep, frying pan, heat the oil with 20 g of the butter and sauté the onions, carrots and celery, all finely chopped, over a gentle heat for 5 minutes. Add the rice and stir it over a high heat for 2 minutes.

Moisten with the wine, allow to evaporate, then pour in the first ladleful of very hot stock. Stir well. Add the chicken and the sage leaves. Continue to cook for 15 minutes over a medium heat, pouring in more hot stock as soon as the previous ladleful is almost absorbed. Stir frequently.

Adjust the seasoning. Off the heat, add the rest of the butter and the parmesan. Cover and allow to rest for 2 minutes. Serve *all'onda*, which is to say, still fluid.

The authentic recipe

I have simplified here a recipe from Veneto, where the risotto is made using a whole boned chicken cut into small pieces. The meat is sautéed with the vegetables and the rice is added halfway through the cooking.

My suggestion

This risotto is ideal for a one-dish meal or to warm up a cold day!

Risotto *con Prosecco e pistacchi*

Risotto with Prosecco and pistachios

For 6 people
Preparation time: 15 minutes
Cooking time: 30 minutes

For the Prosecco sauce

150 g French shallots, finely chopped
20 g butter
250 ml Prosecco white sparkling wine
salt

90 g butter
120 g unsalted pistachios
100 g French shallots, chopped
2 tablespoons olive oil
500 g carnaroli rice
150 ml Prosecco white sparkling wine
salt
1.6 litres chicken or vegetable stock
60 g parmesan cheese, grated

Preparation

For the sauce, sauté the shallots in the butter over a very low heat, with 2 tablespoons of water. After 5 minutes, pour in the Prosecco and reduce to a creamy consistency. Season with salt and mix in.

In a frying pan, heat 10 g of the butter and brown the pistachios in it, then crush them.

In a heavy-based saucepan, sauté the shallots for 5 minutes with the olive oil and 20 g of the butter. Pour in the rice, stirring over a high heat for 2 minutes. Moisten with the Prosecco, allow to evaporate, then season with salt. Add the hot stock gradually, ladleful by ladleful, stirring frequently.

As soon as the risotto is ready, mix in half the pistachios off the heat then the remaining butter and the parmesan. Combine, cover and allow to rest for 2 minutes. Serve the risotto with 1 spoonful of sauce in the middle of each plate and scatter with pistachios.

My pet ingredient

Prosecco is the wine from the hills of Treviso (the town of my birth) and it is renowned throughout the world. It is a sparkling white wine, both dry and floral. The Italian 'Champagne', in a sense. It has become the national apéritif.

ARANCINI

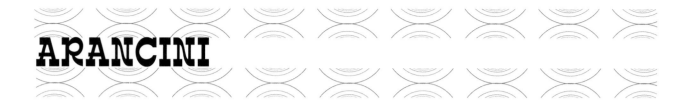

For 6 people
Preparation time: 1 hour
Cooking time: 1 hour

150 g peas
300 g bolognese ragù (see recipe page 133)
300 g risotto rice
salt
50 g butter
50 g parmesan or pecorino cheese, grated
1 sachet ground saffron
3 eggs
200 g plain (all-purpose) flour
200 g breadcrumbs
2 litres oil for deep-frying (olive or peanut)
1 tablespoon chopped parsley
1 tablespoon chopped basil

Preparation

Add the peas to the bolognese ragù in a saucepan and cook over heat until they are tender. Drain the ragù and set aside the liquid (if there is any).

Cook the rice until *al dente* in boiling salted water, drain and add the butter, parmesan and the saffron diluted in the ragù liquid (or in a little water). Allow to cool before adding 1 of the eggs, the chopped basil and parsley.

Have all the ingredients ready: the rice, the ragù, the flour, the remaining eggs (beaten), the breadcrumbs, water for moistening your hands and trays dusted with breadcrumbs for the arancini before they are deep-fried.

Take a small quantity of rice with your right hand and place it in your left hand, moistened with water. Shape into balls the size of a small orange (arancino), make a hole in the middle and put a little ragù inside. Cover over with rice.

Roll the balls in the flour, then in the beaten egg and finally in the breadcrumbs. Place on the trays.

Plunge the arancini (no more than 4 or 5 at a time) in the very hot oil, in a deep saucepan. Drain them immediately on paper towels. Serve hot.

Variations

You can replace the meat with a stretched-curd cheese (mozzarella, caciocavallo or scamorza) and mashed hard-boiled eggs.

trattoria

Carpaccio **del manzo**

Beef carpaccio

This dish was created in the sixties in Venice, on the occasion of an exhibition of the Venetian painter Carpaccio, some of whose reds were reminiscent of the colour of meat.

For 6 people
Preparation time: 10 minutes

500 g beef fillet
olive oil
salt, pepper

Preparation

Arrange the beef sliced ultra-thin on six plates, brush with a little olive oil and cover with plastic wrap. Keep in the fridge until serving time. Season with salt 5 minutes before eating and serve with a dressing of your choice.

Rocket and parmesan cheese
Arrange a handful of rocket (arugula) dressed with olive oil and lemon on the beef. Garnish with shavings of parmesan.

Balsamic vinegar
Reduce 200 ml balsamic vinegar over a gentle heat until you have a thick syrup. Dress the carpaccio with this sauce and serve with a rocket salad.

Taggiasca olives
Scatter the beef with chopped basil and cover with finely chopped black olives.

Mayonnaise and mushrooms
Spread a thin layer of dijonnaise and garnish with thin slices of mushroom.

Cipriani sauce
Combine 150 g mayonnaise with 3 tablespoons of pouring cream, 5 tablespoons of tomato passata (puréed tomatoes), 1 teaspoon mustard, 2 tablespoons of Worcestershire sauce and 1 pinch salt.

Celery and black truffle
Dress the carpaccio with olive oil and balsamic vinegar, garnish with matchsticks of celery and slivers of black truffle.

My suggestion

Have your butcher slice the meat. Provide a plate on which he can present it.

Variation

In the 'tagliata' version, the meat is a little thicker, marinated in olive oil flavoured with rosemary and briefly seared on a very hot grill (just a moment on each side). Serve with rocket dressed with balsamic vinegar and parmesan cheese.

VITELLO ALLA MILANESE
LA MILANESE

Milanese-style veal

For 6 people
Preparation time: 20 minutes
Cooking time: 30 minutes

6 thin escalopes of veal
2 eggs
breadcrumbs
40 g butter
60 ml olive oil
salt
2 lemons

Preparation

Ask your butcher to flatten the escalopes. Beat the eggs in a shallow dish, pour the breadcrumbs onto another plate. Dip the escalopes into the beaten egg then in the breadcrumbs, pressing firmly so that the mixture sticks.

Melt the butter with the oil in a heavy-based frying pan and cook the escalopes in it, two or three at a time. When the crumb coating is golden, take them out and dry on paper towels. Season with salt. Serve hot with quarters of lemon or cold with a tomato salad.

My suggestion

In summer, you can take these escalopes cold to a picnic.

Variation

Make the escalopes with chicken or turkey breast. You can also deep-fry them in oil.

The authentic recipe

This uses a veal cutlet on the bone, cut from the veal loin. It is quite thick (2 cm) and needs to cook for about 8 minutes on each side.

VITELLO **TONNATO**

Veal with tuna and mayonnaise

For 6 people
Preparation time: 20 minutes
Cooking time: 1 hour

1 kg veal (outside round)
1 onion
1 carrot
1 celery stalk
6 parsley stalks
salt

For the sauce

300 g tuna in oil, drained
6 anchovy fillets
30 g rinsed salted capers
1 handful of parsley, roughly shredded
100 g mayonnaise
salt, pepper

Preparation

Cook the veal by simmering it with the vegetables and parsley stalks for 45 minutes. Allow to cool in the broth.

For the sauce, process the tuna with the anchovies, half of the capers and some parsley, 50 ml of the cold broth and the mayonnaise. Season with salt and pepper. If the sauce is too thick, add a little more broth. Keep in the fridge until serving time.

Cut the veal into thin slices, arrange them on plates, overlapping each by 2 cm, cover with sauce, garnish with capers and parsley.

My suggestion

This dish gets everyone's vote as soon as the first sunny days arrive and it is very practical for a buffet. Prepare it ahead of time and offer it with some rocket (arugula) and baked tomatoes. Keep the cooking liquid for a risotto.

My trick

The meat is better if it is cut very thinly (like ham). If you don't have a special machine for this, ask your butcher to do it for you.

Cosce di pollo CON SPECK E OLIVE

Chicken thighs with speck and olives

For 6 people
Preparation time: 30 minutes
Cooking time: 40 minutes

6 chicken thighs
50 g ricotta cheese
50 g parmesan cheese, grated
3 rosemary sprigs
salt, pepper
18 thin slices of speck
2 tablespoons olive oil
3 French shallots
100 ml dry white wine
150 g black pitted olives, sliced

Preparation

Ask your chicken supplier to bone the chicken thighs and remove the skin. Mix the ricotta with the parmesan and the chopped leaves of 1 rosemary sprig. Season with salt and pepper. Stuff the chicken thighs with the cheese mixture and roll them up in the slices of speck.

Arrange them on an oiled baking tray with the shallots, cut into pieces, and bake at 200°C. After 10 minutes, moisten with the white wine and allow to cook for a further 30 minutes.

Cut the thighs into slices, drizzle with the cooking juices and garnish with the olives. Serve with steamed silverbeet (Swiss chard), olive oil and lemon, or with mashed potato.

Variation

Use lean or smoked pancetta in place of the speck and rabbit instead of the chicken thighs.

Petto di pollo *farcito con peperoni e basilico*

Chicken breasts stuffed with capsicum and basil

For 6 people
Preparation time: 40 minutes
Cooking time: 30 minutes

6 red capsicums (peppers)
2 tablespoons olive oil
1 garlic clove
1 bunch of basil, chopped
salt, pepper
6 chicken breasts

For the sauce

2 bunches of basil
½ bunch of parsley
20 g toasted pine nuts
½ garlic clove, crushed
salt
6 tablespoons oil

60 g alfalfa (sprouted seeds)

Preparation

Grill the capsicums, remove the skin, cut them into pieces and sauté them in a frying pan with the oil, garlic clove, basil, salt and pepper. Discard the garlic clove.

Trim any visible fat from the chicken breasts (set aside the tenders for another recipe) and flatten them between two sheets of baking paper. Place each breast on a 30 cm square of plastic wrap, season with salt and pepper, place 1 tablespoonful of capsicum in the centre. With the help of the plastic wrap, roll up the chicken, forming a ball. Wrap in another layer of plastic wrap. Poach them for about 12 minutes in just-simmering water.

Clean the basil and parsley leaves with a tea towel (dish towel). Process them with the pine nuts, garlic and 2 pinches of salt. Pour in the oil in a thin stream.

Remove the plastic wrap from the chicken, cut the breasts in two and serve dressed with the basil sauce, on the alfalfa sprouts.

Variation

Make a stuffing using the vegetables of your choice, which you can bind with some ricotta, an egg and herbs.

POLPETTE

Meatballs

For 6 people
Preparation time: 40 minutes
Cooking time: 30 minutes

50 g crustless bread
100 ml lukewarm milk
2 French shallots, chopped
10 g butter
olive oil
500 g minced (ground) veal
100 g mortadella, finely diced
1 egg
50 g parmesan cheese, grated
2 tablespoons chopped parsley
salt, pepper
nutmeg
plain (all-purpose) flour
50 ml dry white wine
100 ml beef stock

Preparation

Soak the bread in the milk then mash it to a paste. Sauté the shallots over a gentle heat in the butter and a little olive oil.

In a large bowl, combine the veal, mortadella, mashed bread, shallots, egg, parmesan, parsley, salt, pepper and nutmeg.

Shape into balls the size of a large walnut, flour them and cover with plastic wrap. Chill them to firm in the fridge.

In a non-stick frying pan, brown the meatballs in a little oil. Pour in the white wine and the stock, allow to cook over a gentle heat for 15 to 20 minutes. Serve with seasonal vegetables.

Variation

Deep-fry the meatballs in oil or shape into a meatloaf and cook for 1 hour in a casserole dish with tomatoes.

You can replace a quarter of the veal with lean pork and sausage. Or try meatballs made from 100% pure beef or lamb mince.

For chicken meatballs, process 400 g chicken breast meat and add 250 g ricotta cheese, 1 egg, 30 g grated parmesan cheese, salt, pepper and nutmeg. Serve with a tomato sauce.

Saltimbocca

For 6 people
Preparation time: 15 minutes
Cooking time: 10 minutes

6 thinly cut veal escalopes
   from the inside round
6 slices of San Daniele prosciutto
12 sage leaves
3 tablespoons oil
30 g butter
100 ml dry white wine

Preparation

Cut the escalopes in two, place half a slice of prosciutto and 1 sage leaf in the middle of each. Fasten them in place with a wooden pick. No need to add salt, the prosciutto is already salty.

In a large frying pan, heat the oil and butter well before laying out the escalopes side by side. Allow to cook on a high heat for 4 minutes on the meat side and 2 minutes on the prosciutto side. Keep warm.

Add the wine to the frying pan and scrape the bottom with a wooden spoon. Allow to boil for 1 minute. Pour this sauce over the meat and serve with seasonal vegetables or baby salad leaves.

Variations

You can pre-cook the escalopes, 2 minutes each side, and brown them in the oven with cheese (parmesan, mozzarella, provola) or vegetables (sautéed zucchini, buttered asparagus).

Scaloppine

Flour the meat and brown it in a frying pan for 30 seconds on each side. Allow to cook for 5 minutes on a gentle heat, adding some veal stock (100 to 150 ml) as needed. When all the stock is absorbed, add the juice of a lemon or 100 ml dry marsala. Cook on the heat for a further 1 minute.

Involtini

This is a veal escalope stuffed with vegetables (sautéed artichokes, for example) or minced (ground) meat. They are then rolled into paupiettes, browned in a frying pan and the cooking is finished in the oven (15 minutes at 200°C).

My trick

It's not easy to find very thin escalopes like in Italy (even if you ask your butcher for them). At home, I thin them down myself by flattening them with a tenderiser. If you don't have one, cover the escalopes with baking paper and beat them with the base of a small saucepan. Make some small cuts around the edges so that the meat stays nice and flat when it cooks.

Faraona con la peverada

Roast guinea fowl with peverada sauce

For 4 people
Preparation time: 30 minutes
Cooking time: 1 hour

1 guinea fowl
100 g pancetta, thinly sliced
30 g butter
2 tablespoons olive oil
1 garlic clove, roughly chopped
6 sage leaves
2 rosemary sprigs
150 ml dry white wine
salt, pepper

For the sauce

200 g chicken livers
liver of the guinea fowl
100 g sopressa (2 thick slices)
60 g salted capers
2 garlic cloves
zest and juice of 1 or 2 lemons
250 ml olive oil
150 ml dry white wine
salt, pepper
1 bunch parsley, chopped

Preparation

Cover the inside and outside of the guinea fowl with the pancetta, tie in place with kitchen string.

Heat the butter and the oil in a flameproof casserole dish, add the garlic, the sage and the rosemary, then the guinea fowl, and brown the bird on all sides.

Pour in the wine and allow to evaporate for 1 minute. Season with salt and pepper. Cook in the oven for about 40 minutes at 200°C, basting the guinea fowl frequently with its juices.

For the sauce, chop the chicken and guinea fowl livers, the sopressa, 1 garlic clove and mix together with the zest of one lemon. Heat the oil in a saucepan with the other whole garlic clove (remove it when the oil is hot) and then sauté the chopped liver mixture. Moisten with the wine and cooking juices from the guinea fowl, season with a little salt and a lot of pepper. Allow to cook for 10 minutes on a gentle heat before adding the lemon juice, capers and parsley. Leave on the heat for a further 5 minutes. Cut up the guinea fowl and pour over the sauce to serve with polenta.

My suggestions

I like to serve this sauce with rabbit or game. You can replace the sopressa with eight anchovy fillets and the lemon juice with vinegar, increasing the quantities slightly for a more acidic sauce. It is even better with pomegranate juice. For a smoother sauce, put it through a food mill or food processor.

Zampone (from Davoli)

Zampone **e cotechino**

Stuffed pig's trotter with lentils & spicy pork sausages

These are very tasty cooking sausages which are often served with bollito misto. They go wild for them in northern Italy during the Christmas and New Year festivities. They are often served with lentils, which symbolise wealth.

How to serve them

Serve them hot, cut into slices, with mashed potato, silverbeet (Swiss chard) or spinach, white beans and lentils.

In shops

They are sold pre-cooked, fresh during the Christmas period, otherwise vacuum-packed.

Cotechino is made from 50% combined pork meat and fat and 50% rind. All finely chopped with salt and spices before being stuffed into a cow intestine.

Zampone contains more meat and it is stuffed inside the rind of the pig's hind trotters (zampe).

Musetto, typical of the Veneto region, is a fresh sausage whose main ingredient is pork snout.

Cooking

Sausages sold vacuum-packed are pre-cooked. Check the cooking time on the packaging (about 45 minutes). As the sausage is poached inside its vacuum-pack, be careful not to be burned by the hot gelatin when you open the foil bag.

If you find a fresh sausage, prick it in several places so that it doesn't burst, place it in a saucepan of cold water and let it barely simmer for 2 hours. The water must not boil.

Bollito *misto*

Poached meat and poultry

This is a typical Christmas dish in northern Italy. In restaurants, it is served from a trolley, with all the pieces of meat kept hot in the cooking liquid and carved to order ... I was in awe of it when I was little!

For 8 people
Preparation time: 30 minutes
Cooking time: 3 hours

3 carrots
4 celery stalks
3 large onions studded with cloves
sea salt, peppercorns
1 kg (fairly fatty) beef
500 g veal breast
1 free-range boiling hen or capon
500 g beef tongue
1 small bunch of parsley
2 bay leaves
mostarda and horseradish

Preparation

Pour water into a large saucepan, add the carrots and celery, cut into chunks (reserve 1 stalk of celery), 2 of the clove-studded onions, some sea salt and peppercorns. Bring to the boil. Add the piece of beef and wait for the water to come back to the boil before lowering the heat to a minimum. Skim the liquid several times, cover and allow to simmer for 30 minutes. Add the veal breast and the chicken, allow to cook for at least 2 hours 30 minutes, skimming regularly. To check if well-done, prick with the tip of a fork (it should penetrate easily).

Cook the tongue separately, in boiling water for 1 hour, then another 1 hour in water flavoured with the last onion, the reserved celery stalk and a few stalks of parsley and remaining bay leaf. Allow it to cool a little and remove the skin very quickly.

To serve, place the saucepan on the table, take out the meat and cut it up on a board in front of the assembled company, then return it to the broth. Enjoy with sea salt, mostarda, horseradish and salsa verde.

Salsa verde

50 g crustless bread
8 tablespoons vinegar
1 garlic clove
50 g parsley leaves
50 g celery leaves
50 g capers
50 g cornichons
2 hard-boiled eggs
8 anchovy fillets
100 ml olive oil

Moisten the bread with 5 tablespoons vinegar and allow to soak for a few minutes, then process all of the ingredients with the oil and the rest of the vinegar.

Brasato **al barolo**

Beef braised in red wine

For 6 people
Preparation time: 30 minutes
Cooking time: 3 hours 15 minutes

1.5 kg beef topside
salt, pepper
plain (all-purpose) flour
30 g butter
2 tablespoons olive oil
3 carrots, chopped
3 celery stalks, chopped
3 onions, chopped
2 garlic cloves, chopped
6 sage leaves, chopped
1 rosemary sprig
100 g fatty pancetta, diced
1 bottle Barolo wine (or a good red wine)
1 tablespoon tomato paste (concentrated purée)

Preparation

Season the meat with salt and pepper, flour it and brown for 10 minutes with the butter and olive oil in a flameproof casserole dish. Remove and keep warm.

Add the vegetables, garlic, herbs, and the pancetta to the dish. Sauté for 5 minutes on a gentle heat. Season to taste with salt and pepper.

Simmer the wine in a saucepan for 5 minutes. Return the meat to the casserole dish and wait a few minutes before adding the wine and the tomato paste. Cover and allow to gently simmer for 3 hours on a very low heat, adding a little stock if necessary.

Remove the meat, discard the rosemary and put the sauce through a food processor or food mill. Carve the meat into slices, pour over the sauce and serve with polenta pan-fried in butter or mashed potato.

My suggestion

If the sauce is too thin, reduce it on the stovetop or thicken it with a roux (10 g butter cooked for 1 minute with 10 g flour). Reserve a little of the sauce for flavouring gnocchi or agnolotti.

OSSO BUCO IN BIANCO

Osso buco in white wine sauce

For 6 people
Preparation time: 30 minutes
Cooking time: 1 hour 30 minutes

6 pieces of veal osso buco (shin), 4 cm wide
70 g plain (all-purpose) flour
50 g butter
4 tablespoons olive oil
salt, pepper
1 onion, finely chopped
1 carrot, finely chopped
1 celery stalk, finely choppped
4 desalted anchovy fillets
200 ml white wine
300 ml beef stock

For the gremolata
1 garlic clove
1 bunch of parsley
1 lemon

Preparation

Make some cuts around the edge of the pieces of veal so that they stay flat when they cook. Flour the meat.

Choose a fairly large frying pan so that the meat fits in a single layer. Heat the butter with half of the oil and brown the pieces of veal on both sides. Season to taste with salt and pepper. Drain and keep warm.

Discard the fat. Add the rest of the oil to sauté the vegetables, for 5 minutes. Add the anchovies and stir over the heat so that they melt. Pour in the wine and scrape the base of the pan with a wooden spoon to pick up the caramelised bits on the base. Allow to boil for a few minutes.

Arrange the meat in a single layer in a large baking dish, add the vegetables, pour over the sauce and the stock. Cover with a sheet of buttered foil and cook for 1 hour in a 180°C oven.

Make the gremolata by mixing together the garlic, the parsley and the zest of half a lemon, all very finely chopped.

When the meat is cooked (it should come away easily from the bone), season with the gremolata. Present the veal on a dish and pour over the sauce. Serve with a saffron-flavoured risotto, replacing the porcini mushrooms with 80 g beef marrow.

Variation

Osso buco in bianco is made without tomatoes. If you want to add them, leave out the anchovies. Peel 200 g tomatoes, seed them, chop them roughly and add them to the dish before putting the meat in the oven.

Polenta

Polenta is a typical accompaniment in the cuisine of the north-east of Italy, where corn has been grown for three centuries. In the beginning it was a poor-man's dish but today different ingredients are added to polenta to make it a very indulgent preparation.

It takes a long time

A good polenta takes time, between 45 minutes and 1 hour 30 minutes depending on the size of the grains. It is made using yellow or white cornmeal (the latter very often used in Venice to accompany fish). In northern Italy, it is cooked in an unlined copper cauldron (it's mandatory …) but outside of Italy it's nevertheless permissible to use a heavy-based saucepan. You also need a whisk and a long wooden spoon. If you use a pre-cooked (instant) polenta, which is ready in about 10 minutes, and choose an organic product, they're better. But you must try the authentic version at least once, in order to taste the difference.

Ideas

It can be made with Gorgonzola or other melting cheeses (add the cheese at the end of cooking), with pan-fried sausages, softer salami such as sopressa or speck, or else with sautéed wild mushrooms. Once it cools, cut it into chips, rounds, hearts, slices, wedges, etc and brown them in a frying pan or in the oven with a little butter. Serve as a side dish.

Quantities

You need 1 quantity of cornmeal to 4 quantities of water. For white cornmeal, allow 1 quantity to 6 quantities of water. A serving is about 100 g and you add 10 g salt per litre of water.

For 500 g yellow cornmeal, allow 2 litres water (2.5 litres for a flowing polenta and 1.5 litres for a very stiff polenta). The simplest method is to keep a saucepan of boiling water on the stove and add water as needed to obtain the desired consistency.

If you want a more delicate polenta, halve the quantity of water and make it up with milk. You can also add butter and grated parmesan.

Cooking

Pour the cornmeal into the salted water in a stream when it starts to boil. Stir vigorously with a whisk to avoid lumps, then lower the heat as soon as it starts to bubble (be careful of spatters). Continue cooking, stirring frequently with a wooden spoon, for about 45 minutes. The polenta is cooked when it comes away from the sides of the saucepan. If it is quite firm, spread it on a wooden board (in northern Italy, they use a round board). You can also pour it, just before it stiffens, into a mould that has been dipped in water (so that it unmoulds more easily).

Spezzatino di vitello **AL POMODORO**

Veal and tomato stew

For 6 people
Preparation time: 30 minutes
Cooking time: 2 hours

2 onions
2 carrots
2 celery stalks
1 garlic clove
40 g butter
4 tablespoons olive oil
1.5 kg veal shoulder,
    cut into 5 cm pieces
6 sage leaves
1 rosemary sprig
100 ml dry white wine
800 g canned crushed tomatoes
salt, pepper
125 ml chicken stock

Preparation

Finely chop the vegetables and sauté them briefly in a frying pan with 10 g of the butter and half the oil. In a flameproof casserole dish, brown the meat for 5 minutes with the rest of the butter and oil, then remove and keep warm.

Add the vegetables, sage and rosemary to the casserole dish. Sauté for a few minutes then add the meat. After 2 minutes, add the wine. Reduce the sauce before adding the tomatoes. Cover and allow to simmer on a very low heat for 1 hour and 30 minutes. If the sauce reduces too much, add a little stock or water. Adjust the seasoning at the end of cooking and serve with steaming polenta.

Variations

For a spezzatino in bianco, replace the tomatoes with stock. And you can make this with beef, lamb leg or pork loin, and any herbs or spices you choose. Serve accompanied by seasonal vegetables as well.

Polenta **pasticciata**

Baked polenta

This is a unique dish that you can serve with a salad. My favourite version is made using duck ragù.

For 4 to 6 people
Preparation time: 10 minutes
Cooking time: 1 hour

300 g cornmeal (polenta)
meat ragù
30 g parmesan cheese, grated
30 g butter
salt

Preparation

Prepare the polenta according to the method outlined on page 248 using at least 1 litre of water. Butter a large baking dish, pour in half the polenta to a thickness of 2 cm, add the meat ragù and cover with the rest of the polenta. Sprinkle with parmesan and small pieces of butter. Brown in the oven for 15 minutes at 200°C.

seaside

Insalata *del polipo*

Octopus salad

For 6 people
Preparation time: 30 minutes
Cooking time: 40 minutes

1 kg octopus

For the stock
salt
1 onion
2 celery stalks
1 bunch of parsley
1 bay leaf
6 peppercorns

For the dressing
juice of 1 lemon
salt, pepper
100 ml olive oil
2 tablespoons chopped parsley
1 tablespoon chopped mint
1 garlic clove
3 or 4 celery stalks, diced
250 g green and black olives, roughly
    chopped
1 capsicum (pepper), diced

Preparation

Clean the octopus: empty the head, remove the eyes and rinse the tentacles well to get rid of any sand. Bring some water to the boil in a large saucepan with some salt, onion, celery, parsley, bay leaf and peppercorns. Add a cork stopper to the boiling water (apparently this tenderises the octopus). Hold the octopus by the head and lower it gently into the water. Allow to cook for 30 minutes on a gentle heat after the liquid comes back to the boil (a little longer if it is a very large octopus). Leave to cool in the cooking liquid.

For the dressing, whisk the lemon juice with salt and pepper and incorporate the olive oil. Add the parsley, mint and halved garlic clove (remove it before serving). Pour this sauce over the octopus (after removing it from the cooking liquid) and garnish with the celery and the olives. For extra colour, add the capsicum.

As a carpaccio

Before the octopus is completely cold, place it in a mould with a weight on top or roll it tightly in plastic wrap (like a sausage). Chill for several hours in the fridge. Slice it very thinly to serve as a starter or a main course (in summer). Ideal for a buffet ...

As a salade

Cut the octopus into small pieces and marinate them for 1 hour in the dressing. When serving, add diced cooked potato and some capers.

My suggestion

Keep the (strained) liquid from cooking the octopus to make a seafood risotto.

Pesce lesso

Poached fish

This is a flavoured broth, ideal for cooking bass, bream, cod, hake, monkfish, john dory, salmon, sole, trout etc ...

For 6 people
Preparation time: 15 minutes
Cooking time: 15 minutes

For 1 fish weighing 1.5 kg

20 g sea salt
1 lemon, halved
1 bunch parsley
2 bay leaves
white peppercorns
olive oil

Preparation

Place the cleaned and scaled fish in a pan with lid, cover with cold water and add the sea salt, the lemon halves, the herbs and the peppercorns. Bring to the boil then cook at a bare simmer for 15 minutes (10 minutes for a 1 kg fish, 15 minutes for 2 kg, 20 minutes for 3 kg). Lift out the fish, remove its head and tail and make fillets, removing the skin. Present on a large dish with quarters of lemon, a few leaves of chopped parsley and steamed potatoes. A drizzle of olive oil (a delicate oil from Liguria, for example) and some fine sea salt to season and it's ready.

Steamed, Al vapore

My favourite way of cooking during the week because it's quick and practical. No point flavouring the water. A salmon or cod steak cooks in barely 7 minutes. Then, you season with fine sea salt, fresh herbs and olive oil. Offer quarters of lemon on the side. Following the same principle, try cooking en papillote, it's easy and low-fat.

Pesce **al forno**

Oven-baked fish

For 6 people
Preparation time: 15 minutes, plus 1 hour marinating
Cooking time: 30 minutes

1 bream or scorpionfish weighing 1.5 kg
150 ml white wine
1 garlic clove, chopped
6 parsley sprigs
1 baby onion, sliced into rings
2 tablespoons olive oil
sea salt

In sea water, All'acqua pazza

Make one or two diagonal slashes in each side of the fish, in the thickest part. Marinate for at least 1 hour in the white wine, garlic, parsley and onion. Drain the fish, sprinkle with olive oil and place in a large baking dish. Bake in the oven at 200°C for 30 minutes. Dilute the marinade with the same quantity of water, well-salted (using the sea salt) and pour half over the fish after 10 minutes of cooking. Repeat 10 minutes later with the rest of the marinade and allow to cook for a further 5 minutes.

In the oven, Al forno

You can slash the flesh of large-sized fish and marinate them as described above. Season the inside and outside with salt, also add fresh herbs (parsley, thyme or rosemary), drizzle over some olive oil and bake for 5 minutes at 200°C. Lower the temperature to 180°C. Cook 15 minutes on each side for a 2 kg fish.

Fillets

These are practical for large numbers. Cut them into serving sizes and place them skin side down on a sheet of baking paper. Bake for 5 minutes in a 200°C oven. Then all that's left is to transfer the fillets to a serving dish with some accompanying vegetables.

Fritto misto *di pesce*

Deep-fried mixed seafood

For 6 people
Preparation time: 20 minutes
Cooking time: 15 minutes

1 kg crustaceans, shellfish and small fish, cleaned
plain (all-purpose) flour, salt, lemon
2 litres peanut oil

Preparation

Dry the fish, crustaceans and shellfish well and flour them. Heat the oil in a deep saucepan. Deep-fry the fish and seafood, adding the largest items first. Avoid stirring during the first 30 seconds. Drain on paper towels. Season with salt. Serve immediately with fried vegetables: capsicum, zucchini skins, eggplant, red onion.

Fritto misto

Have a very varied assortment of seafood: small sardines, anchovies, small mullets, whitebait, squid rings, cuttlefish, Mediterranean prawns (gamberi), scampi tails.

My suggestion

To make larger fish more crispy, flour them, holding the fish by the tail, then quickly run them under cold water and plunge them immediately in the oil (be careful of spatters). Use different flours for coating the fish: cornmeal, durum semolina, chestnut or buckwheat flour.

With egg

After flouring the fish, dip them in lightly salted beaten egg. Drain well. Arrange them on a skimmer and slide into the hot oil. Deep-fry small quantities at a time.

sardine agrodolce

Sweet and sour sardines

For 6 to 8 people
Preparation time: 30 minutes,
plus 24 hours chilling time
Cooking time: 30 minutes

1 kg fresh sardines
plain (all-purpose) flour
1 litre + 100 ml olive oil
salt
500 g onions
50 g currants (optional)
50 g pine nuts (optional)
400 ml white wine vinegar

Preparation

Clean the sardines, remove the bones and make into fillets. Dry them well before flouring them. Heat the 1 litre of oil in a deep saucepan and deep fry the sardines in batches. When they are golden, lift them out with a skimmer and allow to drain. Season with salt.

Cut the onions into thin slices. Soak the currants in lukewarm water. In a frying-pan, heat the rest of the oil to brown the onions on a gentle heat. Pour in the vinegar and allow to just simmer for 4 minutes. Turn off the heat and season with salt.

Arrange a layer of sardines in a large bowl, add some of the drained onions, the currants (drained) and pine nuts. Repeat the process several times. Pour over the (hot) vinegar in which the onions were cooked: it must cover the sardines. Cover with plastic wrap and leave in the fridge for at least 24 hours.

My suggestion

Make this recipe using anchovies, small trout, mullet … In Venice, these sweet-sour sardines are found in almost all of the bars to have as a snack with drinks.

ZUPPA DI PESCE

Seafood soup

This recipe will vary according to the region and what's available at the market.

For 6 people
Preparation time: 40 minutes
Cooking time: 40 minutes

For the stock

1 onion, chopped
1 carrot, chopped
1 celery stalk, chopped
2 tablespoons olive oil
2 kg cleaned and scaled fish
    (small red scorpionfish and small mullets)
150 ml dry white wine
200 g tomatoes
parsley sprigs
1 bay leaf
salt, pepper

For the soup

2 tablespoons olive oil
1 garlic clove, peeled
600 g small squid
12 Mediterranean prawns (gambas) or
    shelled scampi
salt
600 g fish fillets
    (bass, bream, mullet, sole)
bread (to serve)

Preparation

In a saucepan, sauté the vegetables in the oil. Add the fish, in pieces, and allow to cook on a gentle heat for 4 or 5 minutes. Moisten with the wine. Allow to evaporate for 1 minute. Add the tomatoes, cut into chunks, the herbs and 2 litres of water. Allow to just simmer for 20 minutes. Put this broth through a strainer, pushing down well on the vegetables and pieces of fish. Return to the heat for 2 or 3 minutes. Season with salt and pepper.

For the soup, heat the oil in a frying pan to sauté the garlic for a few minutes. Then separately cook the squid for 1 minute and the prawns for 2 minutes. Season with salt and keep warm.

Add 2 ladlefuls of hot fish stock to the frying pan, add the fish fillets in one layer and cook them for 5 minutes. Distribute the fish fillets, squid and prawns among shallow plates, pour over the broth and eat with toasted bread.

little vegetable dishes

CAPONATA

This is a sort of agrodolce-style ratatouille typical of Sicily. It is served at room temperature as a starter or side-dish. I also like it on crostini or served with a pasta or rice salad.

For 6 people
Preparation time: 45 minutes
Cooking time: 30 minutes

4 eggplants (aubergines)
100 ml olive oil
salt
handful basil leaves, roughly torn
3 celery stalks
3 onions
100 g olives
2 tablespoons rinsed salted capers
2 tablespoons pine nuts
2 tablespoons currants
4 tomatoes
1 tablespoon sugar
50 ml wine vinegar

Preparation

Wash the eggplants and cut them into 2 cm dice. Sauté these in a non-stick frying pan with 3 tablespoons of the olive oil. Season with salt and set aside.

Wash the celery, chop it into small chunks and drop them for 2 minutes in boiling salted water. Drain and set aside.

Sauté the onions, sliced into rings in 1 tablespoon of oil i n a large saucepan. Season with salt. Add the eggplant and the celery, then the olives, pitted and roughly chopped, the capers, pine nuts and currants. Finally add the tomatoes, peeled, seeded and diced. Allow to cook for 3 minutes on a gentle heat.

Mix together the sugar and vinegar, add to the pan and stir for 4 minutes on a gentle heat. Allow to cool, stir through the basil.

The authentic recipe

The authentic recipe is made with deep-fried eggplant. Cut them into dice, dust them with salt and leave them to degorge for 1 hour in a strainer. Rinse and dry them in a tea towel (dish towel) before deep-frying them.

Melanzane arrostito, *pomodori e mozzarella*

Grilled eggplant, tomatoes and mozzarella

For 6 people
Preparation time: 45 minutes
Cooking time: 30 minutes

4 eggplants (aubergines)
100 ml olive oil
salt
oregano or thyme
250 g tomato sauce (see recipe page 156)
1 bunch of basil
150 g mozzarella cheese
100 g parmesan cheese

Preparation

Cut the eggplants into slices 5 mm thick. Lay them out on a baking tray lined with baking paper, brush with olive oil and season with salt. Place them under the griller (broiler) for about 4 minutes (monitor them to check that they don't burn) then turn them over, sprinkle with oregano (or thyme) and cook for a further 1 minute.

On each slice, place 1 tablespoon of tomato sauce, a small basil leaf, a thin slice of mozzarella and a little grated parmesan. Build up several layers of eggplant. Before serving, bake them for a few minutes in a 200°C oven to melt the mozzarella.

My suggestion

I like to offer this millefeuille of eggplant as a starter, with a small salad. You can also serve it as a side dish.

Variation

Slice the eggplants lengthways and top them as in the recipe above before rolling them up. Heat them in the oven to brown. Serve with drinks.

Parmigiana

In a baking dish, arrange a layer of grilled or deep-fried eggplant, top with tomato sauce with basil and sprinkle over some parmesan. Repeat three or four times and bake in the oven for 15 minutes.

Pasta Norma

Deep-fry diced eggplant (or sauté in a frying pan in olive oil) and serve with penne with tomato sauce, sprinkled with ricotta salata.

torta DI SCAROLA E OLIVE

Endive and olive pie

For 6 people
Preparation time: 40 minutes
Cooking time: 1 hour

For the pastry

3.5 g sachet baker's yeast
1 teaspoon sugar
250 g plain (all-purpose) flour
1 teaspoon salt, pepper
50 g softened butter
1 egg

For the filling

4 tablespoons olive oil
1 garlic clove, crushed
500 g endive, cleaned
100 g black pitted olives, chopped
1 tablespoon rinsed salted capers, chopped
70 g currants
70 g pine nuts
3 tablespoons chopped parsley
salt, pepper

Preparation

Place the yeast in a bowl with 100 ml lukewarm water and the sugar. Allow to rest for 10 minutes before combining with the flour, salt, pepper and butter. Work the dough so that it is quite smooth. Cover with plastic wrap and leave to rise for 1 hour in a warm place.

In a frying pan, heat the olive oil and sauté the garlic, then the endive, cut into strips. Leave on the heat for a few minutes to evaporate the excess moisture contained in the greens. Then add the olives, capers, currants, pine nuts and parsley. Season with salt and pepper. Allow to cook for a further minute before taking the pan off the heat.

Work the dough for 30 seconds and divide it in two. Spread out half to line the base of an oiled dish or tin, add the cooled endive mixture and cover with the rest of the dough. Pinch the edges. Brush the top of the pie with oil and allow to rest for 20 minutes. Brush beaten egg over the pie and cook for 45 minutes in a 200°C oven.

erbazzone Spinach pie

Erbazzone is a dish that's typical of the Emilia region. There are many variations. This one is extraordinary and comes to me from my great aunt Vige.

For 6 people
Preparation time: 30 minutes
Cooking time: 50 minutes

For the pastry

200 g plain (all-purpose) flour
2 tablespoons olive oil
20 g lard or butter
salt

For the filling

1.6 kg silverbeet (swiss chard) or spinach leaves
80 g pancetta, finely diced
2 tablespoons olive oil
  + 1 tablespoon for brushing
1 bunch bulb spring onions (scallions), chopped
2 garlic cloves
50 g butter
salt, pepper
½ bunch of parsley, chopped
80 g parmesan cheese, grated

Preparation

In a large bowl, combine the flour and the olive oil, incorporate the lard or butter by hand with 2 pinches of salt then add the lukewarm water in several stages until you have a ball of dough that isn't sticky. Knead on the work surface for a few minutes. Cover with a clean tea towel (dish towel) and allow to rest for 30 minutes.

Wash the greens and steam them for a few minutes. Drain. In a frying pan, brown the pancetta for 1 minute in hot oil, add the spring onions (including the stems) and the garlic, halved. Allow to cook for 4 to 5 minutes on a very gentle heat. Then add the butter, the greens, with their excess moisture squeezed out, and salt and pepper. 'Dry' the mixture for a few minutes on a medium heat.

Cool the mixture a little before mixing in the chopped parsley and parmesan. Taste and adjust the seasoning.

Roll out half the pastry using a rolling pin, lay it in an oiled tin or dish and pour in the filling. Roll out the rest of the pastry, cover the filling, making folds in the pastry and pinch the edges. Prick the pastry with a fork before baking at 180°C. Allow to cook for 30 minutes then brush the pastry with olive oil. Return the pie to the oven until the top is nicely golden brown.

ASPARAGI Asparagus

To prepare asparagus, peel with a vegetable peeler. Remove all of the hard fibres. Green asparagus is more tender than white asparagus and I don't often need to peel them.

Asparagus sauce

Take a bunch of green asparagus, trim 4 cm from the base of the spear, cut off the tips and set them aside. Cut the stem into short rounds, and sauté them in a frying pan in 1 tablespoon of olive oil and 20 g butter. Season with salt and pepper. They must remain firm. Steam the tips for 3 minutes and sauté them with the stems. Use asparagus prepared this way to dress egg tagliolini, adding some butter and parmesan cheese. You can also use it to fill lasagne or crespelle by mixing it with a parmesan-flavoured béchamel sauce. (For 4 people)

Boiling asparagus

The best way to cook asparagus is by steaming. Otherwise, make up small bundles using kitchen string and stand them up, in boiling salted water, in a large cooking pot, with the tips out of the water.

White asparagus needs between 15 and 25 minutes to cook. Cover them with a tea towel (dish towel) so that they stay hot.

Green asparagus must remain firm. Allow 10 to 15 minutes to cook, no more. If you are going to eat them cold, plunge immediately into iced water: they will stay nice and green.

Asparagus with butter and parmesan cheese

Plunge a bunch of asparagus into a large pot of boiling water and remove them halfway through the cooking. Sauté them lightly in a frying pan with 50 g butter and 70 g grated parmesan cheese. Shake the pan often so that the asparagus browns nicely. Serve with fried eggs or gratinate them by scattering over small pieces of butter and grated parmesan cheese and baking.

White asparagus from the Veneto region is superb (especially the Bassano variety). During the asparagus season (April and May), the region's trattoria offer only a 100% asparagus menu: risotto with asparagus, eggs and asparagus. I have some good memories of it!

Risotto with white asparagus

For 6 people
Preparation time: 30 minutes
Cooking time: 20 minutes
400 g aparagus tips, 1 onion, 1 tablespoon olive oil
400 g vialone nano rice, 100 ml dry white wine,
1.2 litres stock, 40 g butter

Preparation

Cut the asparagus tips into short rounds. Sauté the chopped onion in the oil and butter, in a large saucepan, add the asparagus tips and stir for 3 to 4 minutes. Pour in the rice, stir and continue as indicated in the recipes for risotto, first moistening with the wine, then with the hot stock. When the rice is cooked, add the butter, in pieces, and 50 g grated parmesan cheese. Stir.

Carpaccio
DI CARCIOFI

Artichoke carpaccio

For 6 people
Preparation time: 15 minutes

6 small roman artichokes
1 lemon
50 ml olive oil
fine sea salt, pepper
1 handful flat-leaf (Italian) parsley
100 g parmesan, shaved

Preparation

Using a knife, remove 2 cm from the top of each artichoke, trim the stalks. Remove the toughest leaves. Place the artichokes in cold water with a little lemon juice added.

Cut the artichokes into very thin slices just before serving. Present them on a large dish, drizzle over olive oil whisked with the juice of half a lemon, salt, pepper and parsley. Top with shavings of parmesan.

My suggestion

Serve as a starter or with a beef carpaccio or veal escalopes with lemon.

Tortino **di carciofi**

Artichoke tart

For 6 people
Preparation time: 40 minutes
Cooking time: 1 hour 15 minutes

For the braised artichokes

6 roman artichokes
lemon juice
50 ml olive oil
1 garlic clove, crushed
2 tablespoons chopped parsley
50 ml dry white wine
salt, pepper

For the shortcrust pastry

200 g plain (all-purpose) flour
salt
100 g butter
1 egg yolk

For the filling

150 g ricotta cheese
80 g parmesan cheese, grated
3 eggs
100 ml pouring cream
salt, pepper, nutmeg

Preparation

Using a knife, remove 2 cm from the top of the artichokes, trim the stalks. Remove the toughest leaves. Place the artichokes in cold water with some lemon juice added.

Heat the oil in a heavy-based saucepan, add the garlic and parsley. Gently sauté. Arrange the artichokes in the pan, head down, and pour in the wine. Allow to evaporate before adding 50 ml water. Season with salt and pepper. Cover and allow to cook for 20 to 30 minutes on a gentle heat so that the artichokes are quite tender.

Prepare the dough in a mixer, mixing the flour with a pinch of salt and the cold butter in pieces for 30 seconds. Add the egg yolk and 70 ml cold water. Mix for a further few seconds. Bring the dough together into a ball on the work surface but don't knead it too much. Cover with plastic wrap and chill in the refrigerator for 1 hour.

Mix together the ricotta, parmesan, one of the eggs, salt and nutmeg. In a separate bowl beat the cream with the remaining eggs, salt and pepper.

Knead the dough for a scant minute so that it rolls out easily. Make a round of pastry and lay it in a buttered and floured tart dish or tin. Pour in the ricotta mixture, arrange the cooked artichokes on top, head down, opening the leaves out a little, top with the egg–cream mixture. Cook for 45 minutes in a 200°C oven.

Radicchio *di Treviso*

Red Treviso late-season radicchio

The late-season Treviso radicchio is a winter chicory that grows in the areas around Treviso and Venice. It is very labour-intensive to grow, which is the reason for its high price.

Tips for buying

Approach a good greengrocer and order a case to share with your friends. And be sure to make it clear that you want late-season radicchio, not to be confused with early-season radicchio or 'red lettuce' as it is called in France (in Italian rossa di Verona or di Chiogga).

How to clean it

Leave on 1 cm of the root and clean it with a knife. Cut the radicchio lengthways, into four or six. Wash and dry well. If you are using it in a salad, cut the section close to the root into four or five strips.

As a salad

Radicchio has a beautiful shape and pretty colour. It is crisp, with a slightly sweet taste and a pleasant note of bitterness. For the dressing (for 2 people), dissolve 2 pinches of salt in 1 tablespoon good wine vinegar or balsamic vinegar, pour over 2 or 3 cut-up radicchio flowers, sprinkle over 4 tablespoons of olive oil and pepper. Mix well. Serve immediately.

Grilled radicchio

Cut into two or four lengthways, wash and dry. Marinate it for a few minutes in some olive oil with salt and pepper. Grill on a cast-iron plate or in a frying pan. Brush with olive oil and cook on the other side. Brush the red leaves as well so that they don't burn. As a side dish, allow one radicchio flower per person.

Radicchio sauce

For six people, preparation time 15 minutes, cooking time 10 minutes.

Wash 4 radicchios, chop the leaves into 3 cm pieces and the base into small dice. Gently sauté 1 chopped onion in 1 tablespoonful of olive oil and 30 g butter. Add the radicchio and cook on a high heat. When it changes colour, moisten with 100 ml red wine. Season with salt and pepper. Cook for a further few minutes.

Use this sauce to dress pasta with butter and parmesan, a risotto (add the sauce 10 minutes before the end of cooking), lasagne (or crêpes) gratinated with a parmesan-flavoured béchamel sauce or a frittata. Purée the sauce to serve alongside meat or as a dip with drinks.

Rosso di Treviso Precoce
(Cichorium Intybus L. Silvestre)

Variegato di Castelfranco
(Cichorium Intybus L. Foliosum)

Rosso di Treviso Tardivo
(Cichorium Intybus L. Silvestre)

Rosso di Verona
(Cichorium Intybus L. Silvestre)

Bianco di Chioggia
(Cichorium Intybus L. Foliosum)

Rosso di Chioggia
(Cichorium Intybus L. Silvestre)

Enciclopedia del Radicchio.

Il Radicchio dalla A alla Zeta
dal 17 al 30 novembre.

Il buon mercato.

pomodori *gratinati*

Baked tomatoes

For 6 people
Preparation time: 30 minutes
Cooking time: 30 minutes

10 tomatoes
salt, pepper
10 anchovy fillets
100 ml olive oil
1 garlic clove
100 g breadcrumbs
1 bunch of basil
½ bunch of parsley, chopped
2 tablespoons chopped oregano
80 g parmesan cheese, grated

Preparation

Cut the tomatoes in two horizontally, seed them, season the inside with salt and place them upside down on a tray so their liquid drains out.

In a frying pan, gently 'melt' the anchovies with 1 tablespoon of the olive oil and the garlic, halved (remove it afterwards). Off the heat, add the breadcrumbs, herbs, parmesan and 6 tablespoons olive oil. Mix well.

Stuff the tomatoes with the anchovy mixture, drizzle over some oil and bake for about 30 minutes in a 180°C oven. Serve as a side dish.

My suggestion

In summer, serve these tomatoes lukewarm or cold. They go well with spaghetti with olive oil (cut them into four), a vitello tonnato, grilled tuna or swordfish.

PANZANELLA

Tuscan bread salad

For 6 people
Preparation time: 20 minutes

12 slices stale bread with a dense crumb
5 tablespoons wine vinegar
250 ml olive oil
salt, pepper
1 or 2 red onions
1 kg cherry tomatoes
1 celery heart
2 small cucumbers
100 g rinsed salted capers
150 g black pitted olives
1 bunch of basil
50 g caper berries

Preparation

Place the bread in a large bowl. In another bowl, combine 400 ml water with 3 tablespoons of the vinegar, 100 ml of the olive oil, salt and pepper. Pour this dressing over the bread and allow it to swell. If there is not enough liquid, add a little more olive oil or water.

Slice the onion into thin rings and rinse them under running water several times to make their flavour less strong. Cut the tomatoes in half and the celery heart into small pieces. Peel the cucumbers, split them lengthways, remove the seeds and slice the flesh into semi-circles.

Combine the raw vegetables with the capers, olives and some hand-torn basil. Season with 100 ml of the olive oil, the rest of the vinegar, salt and pepper.

In a large bowl, alternate a layer of bread and a layer of vegetables. Finish with the vegetables and the caper berries. Allow to rest for 1 hour at room temperature. Dress with a drizzle of olive oil before serving.

My suggestion

Add some tuna in oil, anchovies, grilled capsicum.

Express version

If you don't have any stale bread, toast some slices of fresh bread, drizzle over some vinegar and olive oil, crush some very ripe tomatoes on top, add some olives, capers, oregano, vinegar, salt and pepper. It's ready!

peperoni **farciti**

Stuffed capsicums

For 6 people
Preparation time: 15 minutes
Cooking time: 40 minutes

2 yellow capsicums (peppers)
2 red capsicums (peppers)
2 green capsicums (peppers)
12 anchovy fillets
60 g rinsed salted capers
60 g black pitted olives
2 tablespoons oregano
12 tablespoons white wine
12 tablespoons olive oil
12 teaspoons breadcrumbs
salt, pepper

Preparation

Cut the capsicums in two, hollow them out and place them on baking tray, lined with baking paper.

Top each capsicum half with 1 anchovy fillet cut in two, 5 or 6 capers, 2 or 3 black olives, 2 pinches of oregano, 1 tablespoon of white wine, 1 of olive oil and 1 teaspoon of breadcrumbs. Season with salt and pepper to taste.

Brown the capsicums for 30 to 40 minutes in a 180°C oven. The flesh should be soft and the filling golden.

My suggestion

Serve as a starter with a salad or to accompany tuna, swordfish or sardines. You can chop the stuffed capsicums and mix them through pasta.

Peperoni ammollicati

Roughly chop 6 capsicums of different colours. Sauté them in a frying pan with 100 ml olive oil, stirring often. Season with salt and pepper. When they are soft, add 150 g fresh breadcrumbs from a country-style loaf, 2 tablespoons of grated pecorino or parmesan cheese, and the same quantity of salted capers, rinsed and chopped.

Frittata
DI ZUCCHINE

Zucchini frittata

For 6 people
Preparation time: 20 minutes
Cooking time: 15 minutes

3 zucchini (courgettes)
3 tablespoons olive oil
1 garlic clove, crushed
salt, pepper
12 eggs
50 g parmesan cheese, grated
1 bunch of basil, chopped

Preparation

Slice the zucchini into rounds. Heat 2 tablespoonfuls of the olive oil in a frying pan (cast-iron if possible), add the garlic then the zucchini. Allow to cook on a high heat for a few minutes, stirring frequently. Season with salt and pepper.

In a large bowl, quickly beat the eggs with a fork, add the parmesan, basil, salt and pepper. Pour over the zucchini and cook at quite a high heat, shaking the pan frequently.

When the eggs start to stick to the sides, pull them towards the centre with a wooden spoon. As soon as the bottom sets, place a large plate over the pan and quickly tip over the frittata.

Add the remaining oil to the frying pan and slide the frittata back in to brown it on the other side. It should be golden on the outside and creamy on the inside. With a little practice, you will get there.

Variation

For this recipe, you can use any vegetable you like: sautéed artichokes, peas, green asparagus, capsicum (pepper). Serve hot as a meal, or cold for a picnic or buffet.

My personal trick

For successful frittata, I use a cast-iron frying pan specially reserved for this purpose. I wash it in water, simply wipe it with paper towels, then I wrap it, well oiled, in some paper. My frittata are perfect and never stick.

fagioli Beans

Borlotti

These are a pinkish white colour, with purple marbling. They are very tasty, especially the Lamon variety from Veneto (you can order them from Italian grocers). When they are dried, they are soaked overnight and cooked for 2 or 3 hours in water. Then they are used in soups, salads, with pasta. For fresh borlotti beans, you need to reduce the cooking time. And if you are very short on time, prepare your dishes with canned borlotti beans.

Borlotti bean and radicchio salad

Combine borlotti beans with some Treviso radicchio (or baby rocket (arugula) leaves) and a well-flavoured vinaigrette.

Bean and tuna salad

Combine canned tuna in oil with some beans, thin onion rings, rocket and vinaigrette.

Bean salad with anchovies

Melt anchovies in a garlic-flavoured olive oil, add some wine vinegar, reduce and pour this mixture over the beans. Wait for 10 minutes before eating.

Cannellini

These beans are all white, and they have a more delicate flavour than borlotti beans. They are cooked in the same way. They are often used to add substance to a soup, such as minestrone. They are enjoyed as a salad with a fruity olive oil and some pepper. You can also try them puréed with olive oil to serve with pan-fried Mediterranean prawns (gambas).

Tuscan-style cannellini beans

Peel some tomatoes and chop them into chunks for sautéeing in a little oil with some garlic and sage. Add cooked cannelini beans and allow to simmer for 20 minutes.

Pasta E FAGIOLI

Pasta and bean soup

For 6 people
Preparation time: 15 minutes
Cooking time: 3 hours

300 g dried borlotti beans
pinch of bicarbonate of soda or small piece
  kombu
1 onion, finely chopped
1 garlic clove, finely chopped
1 celery stalk, finely chopped
1 carrot, finely chopped
100 ml olive oil
salt, pepper
200 g tagliatelle

Preparation

The night before you are gong to use them, place the beans in a large bowl, cover with plenty of water and allow them to soak for at least 12 hours, with a pinch of bicarbonate of soda or a piece of kombu seaweed to make them more digestible.

In a saucepan, sauté the garlic and vegetables in 50 ml of the olive oil. Add the drained beans, cover with cold water and bring to the boil. After it comes to the boil, allow to barely simmer for 2 hours 30 minutes, uncovered. If the water evaporates, add some more (boiling). Season with salt when the cooking is almost finished.

Put half of the beans through a food processor or food mill to make a thick soup. Return to the saucepan and heat before serving. When it starts to boil, add the pasta and cook for the time indicated on the packet.

Serve and allow to cool a little. Use the remaining olive oil and some pepper to season.

The authentic recipe

In Veneto, a ham bone or 100 g rind is added to the cooking water for the beans (it is removed when they are soft) or else the vegetables are sautéed with some pancetta. Instead of pasta, the Venetians like to use rice or barley.

MINESTRONE

A good vegetable soup whose ingredients change with the rhythm of the seasons and your desires. It is even better reheated.

For 6 people
Preparation time: 30 minutes
Cooking time: 40 minutes

1 onion, finely chopped

150 ml olive oil

2 carrots, chopped

2 celery stalks, chopped

2 zucchini (courgettes), chopped

2 potatoes, chopped

the green part of 6 silverbeet (Swiss chard) leaves, chopped

3 fresh tomatoes, peeled and seeded, chopped

100 g green beans, chopped

600 g cannellini beans
   or 200 g dried beans

salt, pepper

2 tablespoons chopped parsley

Preparation

In a large saucepan, sauté the onion in 100 ml of the olive oil. Add the vegetables (except for the parsley), the fresh beans (if they are dry, cook them beforehand) and water to cover.

Allow to simmer on a gentle heat until the vegetables are soft. Purée half of the vegetables and return them to the soup. Season with salt and pepper.

Serve sprinkled with parsley, parmesan cheese is optional. A drizzle of olive oil, some pepper and it's ready.

My suggestion

You can add pasta, but it's not mandatory, or you can instead add some toasted bread, rice or just a drizzle of olive oil. In summer, you can add 2 or 3 tablespoonfuls of basil pesto.

TIMBALLO **DI CAVOLO FARCITO**

Stuffed cabbage timbale

For 6 people
Preparation time: 30 minutes
Cooking time: 1 hour

1 curly green cabbage
200 g arborio rice
50 g butter
1 onion, chopped
1 tablespoon olive oil
400 g sausage meat
1 bunch of parsley, chopped
80 g parmesan cheese, grated
1 egg
salt, pepper

Preparation

Cook the whole cabbage by steaming or boiling in salted water. Allow about 30 minutes so that the heart is tender.

Cook the rice until very al dente in boiling salted water, drain and stir in 30 g of the butter.

In a frying pan, brown the onion for 2 minutes in the olive oil then add the sausage meat. Allow to cook for 3 minutes.

Drain the cabbage and remove the outer leaves. Set them aside. Chop the cabbage heart, mix with the rice, sausage meat, parsley, parmesan and the egg. Season with salt and pepper.

Butter a charlotte mould, line the base with a cabbage leaf and add a layer of stuffing. Repeat several times and finish with a cabbage leaf. Cover with buttered foil and cook for 20 minutes in a 200 °C oven. Wait for 5 minutes before serving.

Variation

You can replace the sausage meat with cooked chunks of chicken and use another grain (buckwheat, wheat) instead of rice.

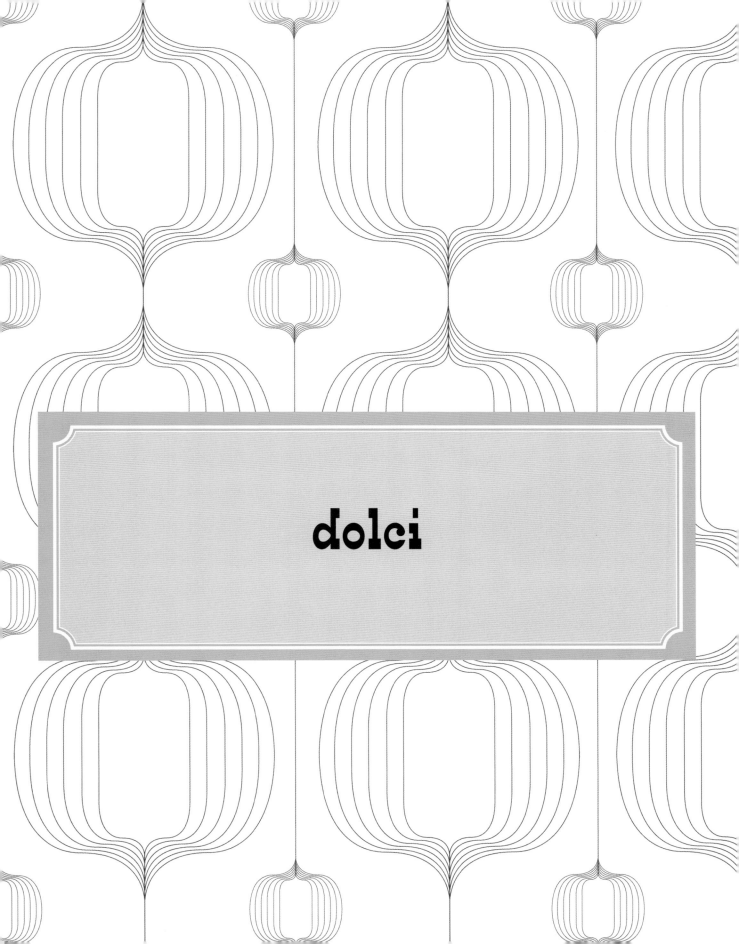

dolci

Traditionally made pannetone (from Rita's)

Panettone e pandoro

In Italy, panettone is reserved for Christmas celebrations. And everybody buys it ready-made (it takes too long to make). It is originally from the Milan region. It is a kind of brioche filled with sultanas, orange peel and candied citron with a sugar glaze and toasted almonds.

Pandoro was born in Verona. It has the shape of a star and is also served at Christmas time. There is no candied fruit in this brioche, which is served in slices to be eaten plain (it is delicious dipped in café au lait) or with sweet sauces at the end of a meal. It can also be filled with a sabayon cream.

Serving ideas

Puréed mostarda and mascarpone which is spread on a slice of panettone. A delicious treat that comes to us from Veneto.
Liqueur or rum-flavoured sabayon.
Crème anglaise and mixed berries.
Chocolate sauce.
Soft or brittle nougat, with almonds, hazelnuts or pistachios. A real Christmas dessert.

My suggestion

Discover traditionally made panettone. Leave it for a few hours (in its packet) near a heat source. It will be even better.

Crostata **di ricotta**

Ricotta tart

For 8 people
Preparation time: 30 minutes
Cooking time: 40 minutes

1 quantity shortcrust pastry (see recipe
   page 345)
50 g currants
plain (all-purpose) flour
500 g ricotta cheese
2 eggs
40 g butter, melted
150 g sugar
50 g pine nuts
1 teaspoon cinnamon
grated zest of 1 lemon
100 ml marsala

Preparation

Lay the pastry into a round tin or dish and chill. Soak the currants for 10 minutes in a bowl of lukewarm water, drain them completely and coat in flour. Beat the ricotta with a wooden spoon before adding the eggs, the melted butter, sugar, pine nuts, currants, cinnamon, lemon zest and marsala.

Pour this mixture into the pastry case and cook for 40 minutes in a 160°C oven. If the top starts to brown too much, cover it with foil.

Variations

From the north to the south of Italy, everyone has their own recipe for ricotta tart. Mine is simple and flavoursome. Flavour it according to your taste with orange zest, candied citrus peel, candied ginger, orange flower water …

For a more delicate tart, mix the ricotta with the sugar and 5 egg yolks, then carefully incorporate 200 ml whipped cream. Beat the egg whites to soft peaks with a pinch of salt and 50 g sugar, mix them into the ricotta and add 250 g raspberries. To cook, allow 1 hour 30 minutes at 150°C.

TORTA **DI CIOCCOLATA**

Chocolate cake

For 6 to 8 people
Preparation time: 30 minutes
Cooking time: 30 minutes

100 g good-quality cooking chocolate
120 g butter, at room temperature
70 g crunchy amaretti biscuits (see recipe
    page 316)
3 eggs
150 g caster (superfine) sugar
50 g plain (all-purpose) flour
1 teaspoon baking powder

For the topping
100 g good-quality cooking chocolate
100 ml cream
70 g toasted almonds

Preparation

Place chocolate and butter in a heatproof bowl over a pan of gently simmering water, stirring until chocolate and butter are melted and combined. Preheat the oven to 180°C.

Process the amaretti in a food processor until they resemble breadcrumbs. Grease a round cake tin with the rest of the butter, line the base and the sides with the crushed amaretti and place the tin in the fridge.

Whisk the eggs with the sugar. When the mixture becomes frothy, gently mix in the flour and the baking powder, then the (cooled) melted chocolate.

Pour this mixture into the tin and bake in the oven for 25 minutes. To test, insert the point of a knife into the centre of the cake: it should come out clean. Allow the cake to cool before turning it out onto a wire rack.

For the topping, melt the chocolate with the cream in the top of a double-boiler. Pour over the cake, spreading it with a flexible spatula. Decorate with crushed almonds if you wish.

Variation

Decorate the cake with nocciolini (little hazelnut biscuits).

My suggestion

Choose a good fondant chocolate, at least 60% cocoa. Serve with chantilly cream or crème anglaise.

CAPPUCCINO CREMA

Cappuccino cream

For 6 people
Preparation time: 30 minutes
Cooking time: 10 minutes
Refrigeration time: 3 hours

3 teaspoons gelatine
200 ml milk
110 g sugar
1 vanilla bean
4 egg yolks
50 ml strong coffee
250 ml cream, very cold

Preparation

Soak the gelatine leaves for 15 minutes in cold water. Bring the milk to the boil with half the sugar and the vanilla bean split in two (discard it afterwards after scraping out the seeds).

Whisk the egg yolks and the remaining sugar until you have a mousse-like cream. Pour in the boiling milk in a stream with the coffee, stirring constantly. Cook in the same way as a crème anglaise (see page 347) for 5 minutes in a double-boiler: the mixture should coat the spoon.

Drain the gelatine well and whisk it into the hot cream. Allow to cool, stirring frequently.

Whip the cream. When the coffee cream mixture starts to thicken, gently incorporate the whipped cream. Pour the mixture into small ramekins or dariole moulds lined with plastic wrap and chill to set for at least 3 hours in the fridge.

My suggestion

Serve with crème anglaise and decorate with coffee beans.

Panna cotta **di pistacchi**

Panna cotta with pistachios

For 8 people
Preparation time: 15 minutes
Cooking time: 5 minutes
Refrigeration time: 2 hours

6 teaspoons gelatine
150 g raw pistachios
1 litre cream, for whipping
100 g caster (superfine) sugar
1 vanilla bean
4 teaspoons ground cardamom
4 tablespoons sour (amarena) cherries
 in syrup

Preparation

Soak the gelatine for 15 minutes in a little cold water. Toast the pistachios for 5 minutes in a dry frying pan and roughly crush.

Pour the cream into a saucepan with the sugar, the vanilla bean, split in two, the cardamom and half the pistachios. Bring to the boil (on a gentle heat) then take the saucepan off the heat. Add the gelatine, after thoroughly squeezing it dry, and whisk.

Pour this mixture into a dariole mould or ramekins. Allow to cool at room temperature then set the cream for at least 2 hours in the fridge. Unmould onto a plate. Garnish with cherries in syrup and the rest of the pistachios.

Variations

Flavour the panna cotta with whatever ingredients you like and serve with a sauce of your choice.

Add the zest of a lemon to the cream and drizzle a raspberry or strawberry coulis over the panna cotta (purée the fruit with a little sugar).

Flavour the cream with 4 tablespoons of instant coffee and serve with a crème anglaise.

Serve pears in red wine with a cinnamon-flavoured panna cotta (2 tablespoons of ground cinnamon).

Flavour the cream with 10 g pure liquorice (from Calabria) and serve with a crème anglaise.

AMARETTI

This recipe can vary according to the region, but it is not new at all (from perhaps the sixteenth century). The most well known are the amaretti from Saronno (Lombardy) and those from Sassello (Liguria). The first are crunchy, the second very soft.

For 20 crunchy biscuits
Preparation time: 20 minutes
Cooking time: 25 minutes

50 g bitter almonds
   or 2 teaspoons bitter almond extract
100 g caster (superfine) sugar
2 or 3 egg whites
150 g ground almonds
100 g icing (confectioner's) sugar

Preparation

Process the bitter almonds with half the caster sugar. Whip two egg whites into soft peaks with the rest of the sugar. Mix the combined bitter almonds and sugar with the ground almonds and add the beaten egg whites. If the mixture is too stiff, incorporate the last egg white without beating it.

Using teaspoons, place small walnut-sized mounds of mixture on a baking tray lined with baking paper. Dust with icing sugar and bake in the oven for about 25 minutes at 150°C.

My trick

Flavour your tarts and cakes with these amaretti. Process them into crumbs for lining the base of a tin or dish, or use in place of flour in a pastry. I use them for fruit tarts, on the base of the tin and on top, with small pieces of butter. And even in certain savoury recipes, with pumpkin and mostarda.

Try the soft amaretti soaked in coffee and served with tiramisù cream.

Crostata *al mascarpone e lamponi*

Mascarpone and raspberry tart

For 6 people
Preparation time: 30 minutes
Cooking time: 30 minutes

450 g shortcrust pastry (see recipe page 345)
200 g mascarpone cheese
200 g ricotta cheese
1 teaspoon pure vanilla extract
50 g icing (confectioner's) sugar
grated zest of 1 lemon
2 tablespoons sweet dessert wine
300 g raspberries

For the coulis
300 g raspberries
1 tablespoon icing (confectioner's) sugar

Preparation

Precook the shortcrust pastry case in a tin. Allow it to cool completely before filling.

In a large bowl, use a wooden spoon to cream the mascarpone and the ricotta with the vanilla sugar, icing sugar, lemon zest and wine. When the mixture is smooth, pour it into the pastry case. Cover with the raspberries.

For the coulis, purée the raspberries with the sugar. Strain through a fine strainer. At serving time, drizzle over the tart.

Variations

Try it with different fruits. For a strawberry tart, allow 500 g fruit in pieces and 200 g puréed fruit with 1 tablespoon of sugar, 1 teaspoon of lemon juice and the zest of 1 lemon.

castagnaccio

Chestnut slice

I adore eating this cake in winter. Made using chestnut flour, it is easy to make and very fulfilling. It is perfect for breakfast, children love them and they make a great snack.

For 6 people
Preparation time: 15 minutes
Cooking time: 30 minutes

50 g currants
250 g chestnut flour
salt
1 tablespoon sugar
3 tablespoons olive oil
some breadcrumbs
40 g pine nuts

Preparation

Put the currants in a bowl of lukewarm water to soften.

Sift the flour (to avoid lumps) into a large bowl, add a pinch of salt and the sugar, pour in 300 ml water in a stream with 1 tablespoon of the olive oil, mixing the ingredients with a whisk. The batter should be liquid.

Grease a tin with another tablespoon of the olive oil and line with breadcrumbs before pouring the batter in to a depth of 2 cm. Pan-fry the pine nuts and scatter over with the drained and floured currants. Drizzle over the rest of the oil and cook for between 20 and 30 minutes in a 190°C oven. It is normal for the top to crack.

The authentic recipe

In Tuscany, they scatter fresh rosemary over this cake before baking it. In Emilia, an egg white is added and the cake is deep-fried.

Tiramisù ai **frutti di bosco**

Tiramisù with mixed berries

For 8 to 10 people
Preparation time: 30 minutes
Refrigeration time: 2 hours

1 kg strawberries
2 tablespoons caster (superfine) sugar
5 eggs
9 tablespoons icing (confectioner's) sugar
125 ml sweet dessert wine
500 g mascarpone cheese at room
   temperature
salt
50 savoiardi (lady fingers)
300 g raspberries
150 g blueberries
150 g blackberries

Preparation

Make a coulis by puréeing 600 g of the strawberries with the caster sugar. Strain through a fine sieve and thin out with 100 ml spring water.

Break the eggs and separate the yolks and the whites into two bowls. Whisk the yolks with 5 tablespoonfuls of icing sugar. When the mixture is frothy, add the wine then the mascarpone, gently stirring to obtain a smooth cream.

Whip the egg whites until they form stiff peaks with 1 pinch of salt and the rest of the icing sugar. Incorporate them into the mascarpone cream.

Dip the savoiardi into the coulis and line the bottom of a dish. Add half the cream, half the berries (slice the remaining strawberries), another layer of moistened savoiardi and a final layer of cream. Decorate with the rest of the berries. Chill in the fridge for at least 2 hours.

Variations

Make the cream lighter by preparing it with ricotta or a mixture of ricotta and mascarpone. This dessert is even better made with génoise sponge (as on page 328) or fresh sponge fingers.

SEMIFREDDO **ALLO ZABAIONE E TORRONE**

Semifreddo with sabayon and nougat

For 10 people
Preparation time: 30 minutes
Freezing time: 6 hours

200 g torrone (nougat) with almonds
100 g bitter chocolate
4 egg yolks
100 g caster (superfine) sugar
200 ml marsala
500 ml cream, for whipping

Preparation

Roughly chop the nougat and chocolate. Make the sabayon by mixing together the egg yolks, sugar and marsala. Allow to cool.

Whip the cream before mixing with the sabayon.

Oil a large dariole mould (or 10 small dariole moulds or ramekins) and line with plastic wrap. Cover the base with a third of the nougat and chocolate then pour in half of the sabayon cream. Repeat once. Finish with the chocolate and nougat. Freeze for at least 6 hours.

Have the semifreddo at room temperature for 10 to 15 minutes then quickly run the base of mould under a stream of hot water. Unmould onto a plate.

Variations

In Italy, nougat is a Christmas confectionery. Mix it with chocolate chips or replace with crushed amaretti biscuits. In summer, try the semifreddo with mixed berries: mix the sabayon with 400 g mixed berries and 500 ml whipped cream. Set in the freezer and serve with extra berries and coulis (purée extra berries with some lemon juice and sugar).

TORTA ALLA NOCCIOLA

Hazelnut cake

For 6 people
Preparation time: 25 minutes
Cooking time: 30 minutes

250 g hazelnuts
zest of ½ an orange
150 g sugar
3 eggs
120 g butter, softened
150 g ricotta cheese
200 g plain (all-purpose) flour
7 g yeast
milk ·

Preparation

Toast the hazelnuts for 2 minutes in a dry frying pan. When they have cooled, rub them between your hands to remove the skin. Finely chop about 180 g of them. Grate the orange zest.

Beat the sugar with the eggs. Then mix in the softened butter, ricotta and orange zest, then the flour mixed with the yeast, the chopped hazelnuts and a little milk if the mixture is too thick. Mix well.

Pour the mixture into small buttered and floured tins. Coarsely crush the remaining hazelnuts and push them a little into the top of the cake mixture. Cook for 20 minutes in a 180°C oven.

My suggestion

I'm fond of starting the day with this rich cake. Instead of flouring the tins, I prefer to dust them with crushed amaretti. It's delicious …

oli,
ste le
Ma che sia
merevoli
si augura
ad un passo dallo scud
lata dai timori legati all
blico, vive di attualità
programmazione, vis
tenza del Tas le ha co
sibilità di fare mercat
ma estate. Insomma
questa — ammette
letti —. Vanno miglio
cole cose. La situazi
strofica, non è allo s
biamo fare qualch
Più che pensare a
l'esigenza di creare
e allo stad
può essere
vità, dunque.
d al suo posto gio
eja ritorna al modul
con Sosa unico riferimento offensivo ed al-
palle il tridente formato da Capparella,
que andrà a finire, ci
miremo sopra e doma-
ni ci sveglieremo con i pie-
di per terra pensando al
Grosseto. Perché per noi
l'obiettivo primario rima-

Zuppa *inglese*

Trifle

For 6 to 8 people
Preparation time: 40 minutes
Cooking time: 40 minutes
Refrigeration time: 2 hours

250 g génoise sponge (see recipe page 344)
   or 200 g savoiardi (lady fingers)
1 quantity of crème pâtissière (see recipe
   page 347)
80 g good-quality cooking chocolate
   (minimum 60% cocoa)
100 ml rum

Preparation

You can make the génoise sponge the day before. Make the crème pâtissière (see basic recipes p344 for details). While it is still hot, mix half of the crème pâtissière with the chocolate chopped into small pieces.

Cut the génoise into 1.5 cm slices, brush with the rum mixed with 100 ml water and line the bottom of a charlotte mould. Pour over a layer of the crème pâtissière (chocolate or vanilla), cover with the moistened génoise, add another layer of crème pâtissière and finish with a layer of génoise. Chill for at least 2 hours.

My suggestion

You can replace the red liqueur with food colouring. For a more indulgent treat, serve this dessert with a sabayon sauce.

La torta **di compleanno**

Birthday cake

For 8 people
Preparation time: 1 hour
Cooking time: 30 minutes

1 génoise sponge (see recipe page 344)
1 quantity of crème pâtissière (see recipe
   page 347)
80 g good-quality cooking chocolate
   (minimum 60% cocoa)
500 ml cream, for whipping
2 tablespoons icing (confectioner's) sugar
300 ml marsala
coloured decorations

Preparation

You can make the génoise the day before. Make the crème pâtissière. While it is still hot, mix half of the crème with the chocolate chopped into small pieces.

Whip the (very cold) cream with the icing sugar. Mix a third of this chantilly cream with the chocolate crème pâtissière, another third with the plain crème pâtissière and reserve the rest for decorating.

Slice the génoise into three rounds using a bread knife. Brush them with marsala mixed with 100 ml water. Spread a layer of (chocolate or vanilla) crème pâtissière on the first round, cover with another round, spread with the rest of the crème pâtissière and top with the third round spread with chantilly cream. Garnish with decorations.

My suggestion

I decorate this cake with sweets, coloured biscuits, sugar flowers, mixed berries, depending on the inspiration of the moment. You can also use another liqueur instead of marsala.

Variation

Fill the génoise with a sabayon cream and decorate the cake with fresh raspberries.

Noccioloni and nocciolini (from Qualitatlia)

CANTUCCI & VIN SANTO

TIRAMISÙ **CLASSICO**

Classic tiramisù

For 8 to 10 people
Preparation time: 30 minutes
Refrigeration time: 2 hours

500 g mascarpone cheese
8 small cups of very strong, cold espresso
   coffee
5 eggs
7 tablespoons icing (confectioner's) sugar
100 ml marsala
salt
200 g Pavesini biscuits
2 tablespoons unsweetened cocoa (for
   dusting)

Preparation

Take the mascarpone out of the fridge while you make the coffee.

Break the eggs and separate the whites and the yolks into two large bowls. Beat the yolks with 5 tablespoonfuls of icing sugar. When the mixture is frothy, add the marsala then the mascarpone, combining gently to obtain a smooth cream.

Beat the egg whites to stiff peaks with 1 pinch of salt and the rest of the icing sugar. Fold into the mascarpone cream.

Dip the biscuits quickly into the coffee and line the base of a large dish. Add a thin layer of cream, and another layer of dipped biscuits. Repeat the operation twice more, finishing with the cream. Refrigerate for at least 2 hours. Just before serving, dust the tiramisù with cocoa.

My suggestions

Buy Pavesini biscuits from an Italian delicatessen or use savoiardi (lady fingers). You can replace the marsala with amaretto. For children, dip the biscuits in a chocolate-flavoured drink.

Variations

Sprinkle crushed amaretti (about 100 g) over the biscuits, roughly chopped chocolate or unsalted chopped pistachios.

GRANITA **AL CAFFE**

Coffee granita

A memory from holidays in Sicily, granita is perfect for hot days ...

For 6 people
Preparation time: 10 minutes
Freezing time: 4 hours

90 g sugar
700 ml very strong espresso coffee
300ml whipping cream
1 rounded tablespoon icing (confectioner's)
   sugar

Preparation

Make a syrup by boiling the sugar and 300 ml water for a few minutes. Pour into a plastic or stainless steel container with the coffee and allow to cool.

Place it in the freezer to set for 1 hour 30 minutes. Scrape the ice with a fork to make crystals. Freeze for a further 2 hours 30 minutes.

Whip the cream with the sugar. Serve the granita in glasses and garnish with whipped cream.

Lemon granita

Make a syrup with 100 g sugar and 750 ml water. Allow to cool before mixing in 250 ml lemon juice.

Peach granita

Make a syrup with 100 g sugar and 500 ml water. Allow to cool before mixing in 100 ml lemon juice and 250 ml puréed peach.

Zabaglione

For 6 people
Preparation time: 15 minutes
Cooking time: 10 minutes

6 egg yolks
100 g caster (superfine) sugar
150 ml dry marsala

Preparation

Mix together the egg yolks, sugar and marsala in a bowl. Place over a saucepan of just-simmering water (it mustn't boil) and whisk the cream for about 10 minutes to obtain a light mousse. To cool the zabaglione, dip the bowl into iced water and stir frequently (and gently).

Serving ideas

Serve hot or warm in dessert dishes, with dry biscuits, a génoise sponge, slices of panettone or pandoro.

Mix the cold zabaglione with 200 ml whipped cream and serve with fresh fruit.

Zabaglione cream

Whisk 4 egg yolks with 100 g sugar. Incorporate 25 g sifted plain (all-purpose) flour and 250 ml sweet white wine. Bring to the boil, stirring. Allow to cool.

Whip 250 ml cream into a chantilly (cream whipped together with sugar and optional vanilla added) and gently incorporate it into the zabaglione. Chill for 30 minutes in the fridge. Use to fill tarts and cakes.

GELATI

I adore gelati and, like most Italians, I not only eat them in summer, but at any time of the day. They are easy to make with an ice-cream maker, otherwise you need to have time.

There are three types of gelato.

Gelatos with a 'white' base, made using milk, cream and sugar. Fior di latte gelato is a delight. There are many variations: with dried fruit, chocolate (stracciatella, with chocolate chips), hazelnuts, coffee, pistachios or yoghurt, with candied fruit (cassata), etc.

Gelatos with a 'yellow' base are made with eggs. The basic recipe is a (vanilla-flavoured) crema, made in the same way as a crème anglaise.

Sorbets are made using a base of water, sugar and whole fruit purée, juice (lemon).

Sauces for gelato

Chocolate

Melt 200 g dark or white chocolate with 100 ml milk. If you like, add a dash of liqueur or your choice of spices.

Caramel

Combine 100 g sugar and 2 or 3 tablespoons water in a saucepan over heat. When the caramel starts to colour, take the saucepan off the heat, add 250 ml whipping cream. Reheat quickly without allowing it to boil.

Berry

Make a syrup by dissolving 50 g sugar in 150 ml water over a gentle heat. Add 400 g mixed berries and allow to simmer for 3 minutes. When the mixture is cold, purée with 50 ml kirsch liqueur.

Serving

In certain regions of Italy, gelato is served in a brioche (focaccina).

To make an affogato, pour a cup of strong espresso coffee over a scoop of vanilla gelato.

Variations

Flavour the warm cream with 300 g chopped dark chocolate or 3 teaspoons instant coffee.

Storing

Home-made gelato doesn't store well for long, so discard after 2 days.

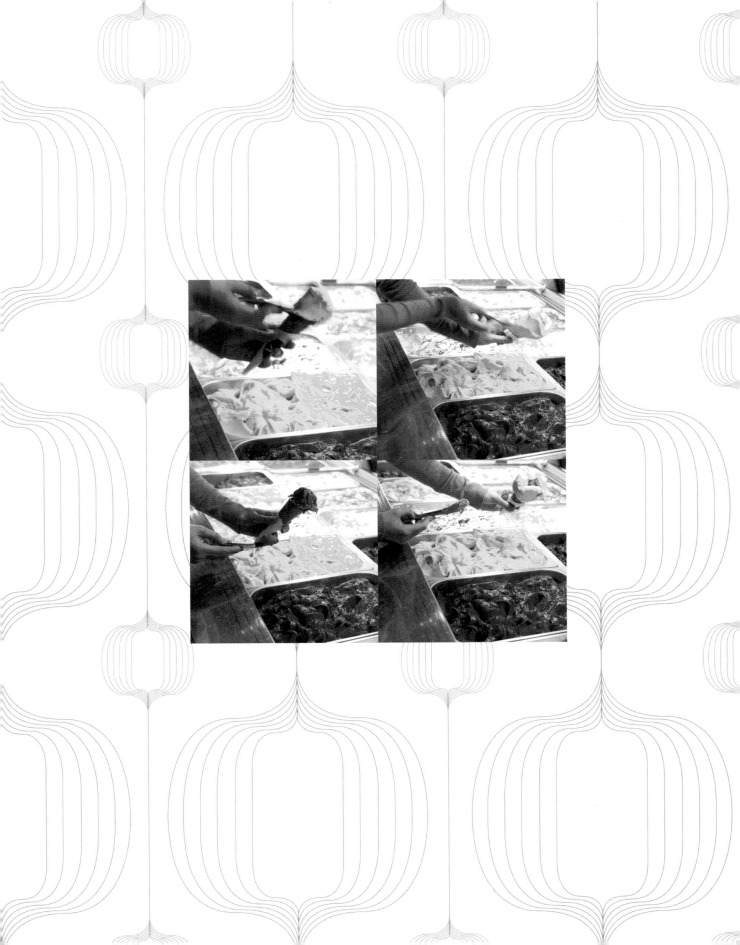

Strawberry sorbet

For 6 people
Preparation time: 20 minutes
Cooking time: 5 minutes
Freezing time: 3 hours

200 g caster (superfine) sugar
600 g strawberries
juice of a ½ lemon

Preparation

Make a syrup by dissolving 120 g of the sugar in a saucepan with 250 ml water. Allow to cool a little. Purée the strawberries with the rest of the sugar and the lemon juice. Set aside a little coulis for serving and mix the rest with the warm syrup. Taste and add a little more sugar or lemon juice if necessary.

Place in an ice-cream maker or freeze for 3 hours in a plastic or stainless steel container, stirring every 30 minutes with a spatula. Serve in quenelles with some coulis and sliced strawberries.

Variations

Sorbets can be made using all kinds of fruit. It is just a matter of adjusting the amount of sugar. For apple or pear sorbets, first cook the fruit then flavour them with a little alcohol.

Crema-based gelato

For 8 people
Preparation time: 20 minutes
Cooking time: 5 minutes
Freezing time: 5 hours

750 ml milk
100 ml cream
1 vanilla bean
zest of ½ a lemon
8 egg yolks
220 g sugar

Preparation

Bring the milk to the boil with the cream, the vanilla bean split in two and the lemon zest.

Whisk the egg yolks with the sugar. Pour over the hot milk (strained) and thicken over a gentle heat, constantly stirring (as for a crème anglaise (please see recipe page 347), but do not let it boil.

To cool the custard, place the container over some ice cubes and stir. Set the gelato in an ice-cream maker or pour it into a container (plastic or stainless steel) and freeze it for 5 hours, stirring it every 30 minutes with a spatula.

Variations

Flavour the warm custard with 300 g chopped dark chocolate or 3 teaspoons of instant coffee.

Storing

Home-made gelato doesn't store for long so discard after two days.

Ricette **elementare** Basic recipes

Pan di Spagna génoise sponge

This 'Spanish bread' was created by an Italian pastry cook during his period spent close to the royal family in Spain, in the middle of the eighteenth century.

For 6–8 people
Preparation time: 20 minutes
Cooking time: 35 minutes

6 eggs
160 g caster (superfine) sugar
160 g plain (all-purpose) flour
1 pinch salt

Preparation

Preheat the oven to 180°C. Cut out a round of baking paper 26 cm in diameter and place it in a sponge-cake tin.

Whisk the eggs with the sugar for 10 minutes to make it frothy. Then incorporate the sifted flour with the salt. Pour into the tin and cook for 35 minutes in the oven. Turn the hot sponge cake out onto a wire rack. Allow to cool completely before filling.

Ideas for using

For charlottes, replace savoiardi (lady fingers) with this Italian sponge cake. It makes a delicious dessert filled with cream.

Salsa di cioccolata chocolate sauce

200 g good-quality cooking chocolate (minimum 60% cocoa)
200 ml cream
50 ml liqueur of your choice (optional)

Preparation

Melt the chocolate in a double-boiler with the cream. Add the liqueur (or spices).

This sauce can be served with semifreddo, panna cotta, vanilla ice cream or pandoro.

Pasta frolla shortcrust pastry

For 450 g pastry
Preparation time: 10 minutes
Resting time: 1 hour
Cooking time: 25 minutes

250 g plain (all-purpose) flour
1 pinch salt
80 g caster (superfine) sugar
120 g (very cold) butter
grated zest of 1 lemon
2 egg yolks
1 tablespoon marsala

Preparation

Place the flour, salt, sugar and the butter in small pieces in the bowl of a mixer. Mix for 10 seconds to obtain a coarse, crumbly mixture. Add the lemon zest. Run the motor and incorporate the egg yolks one by one, then the marsala. Don't process for more than 30 seconds.

Bring the dough together into a ball on the work surface without kneading it for too long. Wrap in plastic wrap and leave in the fridge for 1 hour.

Knead the dough quickly before rolling it out with a rolling pin on the floured work surface. Lay inside a buttered and floured dish or tin. Trim the overhanging edges, folding 2 cm pastry over inside.

Prick the base with a fork. Chill while you preheat the oven (to 180°C).

To precook the pastry, place a circle of baking paper on top, add some dry beans and bake for 12 to 15 minutes. Remove the paper and the beans, return to the oven for 10 minutes to finish the cooking. Finally glaze the pastry with egg white and return it to the oven for 30 seconds to prevent the pastry getting soft from the filling.

By hand

Sift the flour onto the work surface, add the butter (softened) in small pieces and work the mixture with the fingers until it resembles coarse breadcrumbs. Then incorporate the sugar, the lemon zest, the egg yolks and the marsala. Knead the pastry just until it is smooth, but don't over-knead it. Bring it together into a ball, wrap in plastic wrap and place in the fridge.

Crème anglaise

For 6 people
Preparation time: 20 minutes
Cooking time: 10 minutes

500 ml milk
1 vanilla bean
4 egg yolks, at room temperature
80 g sugar

Preparation

Bring the milk to the boil with the vanilla bean split in two. Whisk the egg yolks with the sugar in a bowl. The mixture must become pale. While continuing to stir, pour the hot milk over the egg mixture through a strainer.

Place the bowl over a saucepan of just-simmering water and thicken the custard, constantly stirring with a wooden spoon. It is ready when a finger run through a spoon coated with custard leaves a defined trace. To cool down the custard, dip the bowl into iced water and stir the custard frequently. Use within 12 hours.

My suggestion

Serve this crème anglaise with cakes, charlottes, desserts, brioches (like pandoro). You can flavour it with orange zest, coffee, liqueur or spices.

Crème pâtissière

For 6 people
Preparation time: 20 minutes
Cooking time: 15 minutes

500 ml milk
zest of 1 lemon
1 vanilla bean
4 egg yolks, at room temperature
120 g caster (superfine) sugar
60 g plain (all-purpose) flour
1 pinch salt

Preparation

Bring the milk to the boil with the lemon zest and the vanilla bean split in two. Allow to cool to lukewarm and strain the milk through a fine strainer. Whisk the egg yolks with the sugar in a large bowl. Incorporate the flour and salt then gradually pour in the hot milk, stirring.

Return the mixture to the saucepan and thicken on a gentle heat, stirring constantly. Continue to cook for 3 minutes after it comes to the boil. To cool down the crème, dip the saucepan in iced water. Stir frequently.

My trick

So that none of the vanilla is wasted, scrape the seeds out well with a knife (after cooking) and return them to the saucepan. Dry the bean and crush it with sugar.

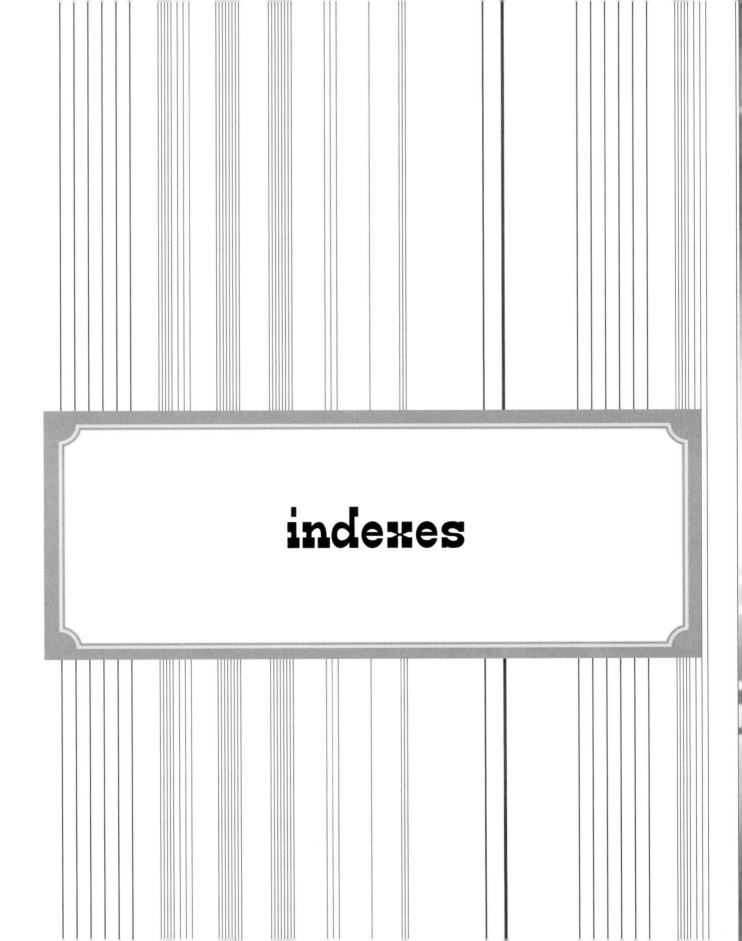

indexes

Menu ideas

Here are a few lists of recipes to help you prepare a menu. As a bonus, a few ideas for outstanding wines (Italian of course) suggested by Rita from Idea Vino (see addresses).

Menu for an Italian Christmas
25 December

Antipasti
Parmesan shortcrust biscuits with truffle-flavoured mascarpone
Hot crostini with lardo di Colonnata
Mini-kebabs of Culatello and artichoke hearts in oil
Wine: Antica Cantina Fratta Franciacorta Brut (Piedmont)
*

Lasagna (or tortelli) with Hokkaido pumpkin
Wine: Gaja's Gaja & Rey (Piedmont).
*

Bollito misto (pot-au-feu) with zampone
Wine: Ceretto Barbaresco Asij (Piedmont)
*

Pandoro, and panettone, mostarda & mascarpone
Or Semifreddo with sabayon and nougat
Or Ceretto Moscato D'Asti (Piedmont)

Seafood Menu

Antipasti
Crostini of polenta with cuttlefish ink
Lingue crispbread spread with caper butter and grated tuna bottarga, mascarpone with anchovies and truffle
*

Octopus carpaccio with celery & taggiasca olives
Or Venetian-style agrodolce sardines
Wine: Cusumano Insolia (Sicily)
*

Spaghetti with clams, or with sea urchins
Or Baked bass (or bream) fillets & caponata

Or stuffed capsicums
Wine: Miceli Chardonnay (Sicily)
*

Cappuccino cream, a Borghetti coffee
Or just a coffee
Or panna cotta and mixed berry coulis
Wine: Banfi Brachetto d'Acqui (Piedmont)

Spring Menu

Antipasti
Lingue crispbread spread with ricotta cheese & basil pesto, ricotta cheese & pistachio pesto, stracchino & rocket, artichoke paste and almonds
Wine: Nino Franco Prosecco di Valdobbiadene (Veneto)
*

Lasagne or (Tortelloni) with artichokes
Or risotto primavera
Wine: Argiolas Vermentino Costamolino (Sardinia)
*

Sauté of veal in bianco
Wine: Umani Ronchi Verdicchio Riserva Plenio (Marche)
Or sauté of lamb in bianco
& green vegetables (asparagus, peas, zucchini, snowpeas)
Wine: Argiolas Cannonau Costera (Sardinia)
*

Colomba (Easter brioche) and zuppa inglese
Wine: Maculan Dindarello (Veneto)

Sunday Menu with Friends

Antipasti
Lingue crispbread with various toppings (olives, sun-dried tomatoes, artichokes …)
Salami platter (Parma or San Daniele prosciutto, coppa, speck, mortadella …)
Antipasti of vegetables in oil with grissini
Wine: Rinaldini Lambrusco Vecchio Moro (Emilia)
*

Pasta timbale with pigeon
Or lasagne bolognese
Or bucatino with amatriciana sauce
Wine: Col D'Orcia Brunello di Montalcino (Tuscany)
*

Platter of cheeses and preserves
Wine: Contini Vernaccia di Oristano (Sardinia)
*

Tiramisù with coffee or dry marsala
Or panna cotta with mixed berries
Wine: Banfi Brachetto d'Acqui (Piedmont)

For a Cold Buffet

Antipasti
Lingue crispbread spread with olive paste, sun-dried
tomato paste, and artichoke paste.
An erbazzone pie (silverbeet (Swiss chard) pie)
Cubes of zucchini frittata
Eggplant-mozzarella rolls
Buffalo mozzarella, rocket, cherry tomatoes
Wine: Mastroberardino Greco di tufo (Campania)
*

Pasta salad with pesto
Conchiglioni stuffed with al dente vegetables
Panzanella
Warm minestrone
Wine: Villa Matilde Falerno del massico bianco
(Campania)
*

Vitello tonnato
Small Milanese escalopes
Caponata
Baked tomatoes
Stuffed capsicums (peppers)
Wine: Miceli Fiammato (Sicily)
*

Tiramisù with mixed berries
Panna cotta with pistachios and raspberries
Crostata with mascarpone & strawberries
Wine: Brachetto d'Acqui
*Coffee granita

Hot Buffet

Antipasti
Piadina cut into squares, stuffed with stracchino cheese
and rocket
Crostini with lardo di Colonnata
Mini-pizzas

Crostini of polenta & Gorgonzola cheese
Artichoke-ricotta tart
Escarole pie
Wine: Umani Ronchi Casal di Serra Verdicchio di Jesi
(Marche)
*

Bolognese or pesto lasagne
Ricotta & spinach crêpes
Pasta al forno
Pasta & fagioli
Wine: Rinaldini Vigna del Picchio (Emilia)
*

Spezzatino (sauté of veal in tomato sauce)
Brasato on polenta
Polpettone (meatloaf)
Salad of baby leaves
Wine: Marcarini Barbera Ciabot Camerano (Piedmont)
*

Platter of cheeses and sharp preserves
of chilli, mostarda figs
*

Tiramisù
Chocolate cake & amaretti biscuits
Birthday cake
Wine: Covital Marsala Extra Vecchio (Sicily)

Super Menu in 30 Minutes

Antipasti
Lingue crispbread spread with olive pastes, butter and
grated bottarga, sheep's milk ricotta cheese and chilli jam
Wine: Contini Vernaccia di Oristano (Sardinia)
*

Spaghetti carbonara with artichokes
Risotto with truffle paste or saffron
Wine: Villa Artimino Carmignano Riserva Villa Medici
(Tuscany)
*

Platter of bresaola, rocket, truffle oil
Wine: Bertani's Secco-Bertani (Veneto)
Beef carpaccio, rocket and parmesan
Veal escalopes with marsala
Wine: Morgante D'Avola (Sicily)
*

Zabaglione and amaretti biscuits
Wine: Covital Marsala Extra Vecchio (Sicily)
Cantucci & vin santo
Badia a Coltibuono Vin Santo (Tuscany)
*

Baba al limoncello
Wine: Badia a Coltibuono Vin Santo (Tuscany)

index

index

MAIL ORDER

Qualitalia

My favourite range: traditionally made Setaro and Martelli pastas, Caponi egg pastas, Tenuta Castello's organic risotto rice, borlotti beans (page 295), cornmeal for polenta. Mario Fongo lingue crispbread (photo 64) and rubatà grissini. Sangiolaro canned fish products: from bluefin tuna ventresca to bottarga.

Terre Bormane white truffle-flavoured oil and 'tartufalba di Morra' truffle paste (page 34) … A wide range of olive oils, balsamic vinegars, traditional vinegar. 'Elena' pitted taggiasca olives, from Liguria, 'La Nicchia' oregano and salted capers from the island of Pantelleria (page 38), pine nuts from Pisa, dried porcini mushrooms. You can order the best cheeses in advance, aged in Italy by Guffanti. In the sweet section, hazelnut cakes from Piedmont, as well as nocciolini (page 332), meringue amaretti or soft amaretti. The cantucci from Tuscany (page 333) and the mini-babas au limoncello are fabulous.
Tel: 01 47 07 11 44
The internet site: www.qualitalia.fr
Bulk and retail sales by mail order. Mrs and Mr Chierici are importers with a passion for Italian products of quality.

Apogei — Online Sicilian grocery

Simona, the creator of Apogei, is 100% Sicilian: she selects the best products from her native land, which are then sold in the best food stores. Here are a few of her 'best': the pistachio pesto from Bronte, the 4 sapori pesto (with dried fruits), the sweetened pistachio cream, the preserves and flavoured honeys from Mr Aurelio Rumia.

The sun-dried cherry tomatoes and the bottled tomato sauce from Pachino (page 155), the hand-minced olive paste, the eggplant caponata and the 'tonnara' tuna from Mr Campisi.

The pasta sauces with squid ink or sardines from Mrs Quattrocchi.

The pastes for spreading from Mr Filippo Finocchiaro such as artichoke-almond, wild rocket, pesto alla siciliana, pesto alla carettiera, green olive pesto and sun-dried tomato.
For the list of retailers, drop Simona a little email: mail@apogei.com.

LITTLE ITALY IN PARIS

Delitaly

23 rue Poncelet, 75017 Paris
Tel : 01 48 88 00 72
Philippe Rebuzzi, a second-generation Italian – 'the second layer, the one that shines!' – he himself says, has created Il Tre and Delitaly, elegant and fashionable spots to indulge one's appetite for Italian delicacies. At Delitaly, a food store and restaurant, try the antipasti with the salami products (page 16), the cheese and truffle flavoured salami, the burrata (page 81), the ricotta salata (for grating), the arancini (page 219), the filled focaccia ... You will also find a wonderful selection of pastas, canned goods, oils, vinegars (page 33), truffle-flavoured products and basic Italian ingredients.

Il Tre (the restaurant)

3 rue de Petits Carreaux, 75002 Paris
Tel : 01 40 13 03 29
At il Tre (pages 165 and 172), try the pizza (page 49), the calzone fritto, the fried pizzette, the pizza bianca with rosemary and olive oil, the burrata, the smoked and grilled scamorza cheese, the fried fish (page 263), the daily specials (spaghetti vongole, orecchiette with broccoli ...)

Casa della Pasta

5 rue des petits-carreaux, 75002 Paris
Tel : 01 42 33 00 72
This is Philippe Rebuzzi's first food store, which opened 15 years ago.

Croccante

138 rue de Vaugirard, 75015 Paris
Tel : 01 47 83 3 7 28
The 'urban chic' style is as appealing as the welcome. I am a fan of their canned fish products (all the cuts of tuna, from the 'buzzonaglia' to the 'tarantello'), of the fresh vacuum-packed piadina romagnola, accompanied by a legendary porchetta (pages 58–59)! Also of the mozzarella & co. which comes from Naples, typical cheeses such as Montasio, the crescenza and some preserves to go with them (leek, chilli, pumpkin). For its home-made pizza and focaccia (pages 46–47, 52)! Thank you, Massimo.

Davoli

34, rue Cler, 75007 Paris
Tel : 01 45 51 23 41 / 01 47 05 20 74
A lovely atmosphere reigns in this shop of Italy of former times (page 100). All the best Salami products come from the native region of the Davoli family. The giant mortadella from Bologna (page 95) is made to order for the shop. You can also find lean and fatty pancetta (page 103), different cured sausages and hams as well as fresh cotechino during the Christmas period (page 238). A good choice of cheeses: fontina, mascarpone-based Gorgonzola, mountain parmesan matured for 32 months (pages 71 and 75). And fresh white truffle when autumn comes (page 35)!

Cooperativa Latte Cisternino

37 rue Godot de Mauroy, 75009 Paris
In his mini-boutique, Sebastiano serves you in his native tongue and in song. Here you will find mozzarella cheese in all its forms (page 78) and fresh cow's or sheep's milk ricotta (page 82) (direct from the cooperative's own production). A good selection of cheeses, including stracchino (page 87), Piave and mild and grating pecorinos. A range of dried herbs (page 41) and dried vegetables. The opening hours and prices are also Italian-style (closed for the siesta).
Other addresses: 17 rue Geoffroy Saint-Hilaire, 75005 Paris
46 rue du Faubourg Poissonnière, 75010 Paris
108 rue Saint Maur, 75011 Paris.

little Italy in Paris

Da Rita

67 avenue du Docteur Netter, 75012 Paris
Tel: 01 43 41 74 92

Rita's advice makes this the right neighbourhood address. You can find a delicious selection of products from Italy and Sardinia, where Rita comes from. A counter loaded with antipasti, good cheeses: parmesan (page 72), Gorgonzola (page 86), taleggio offered with apple mostarda (page 87), focaccia (page 55), grissini and ciappe (page 63). A large selection of oils to be discovered as well as a handy gadget: a mini oil can in stainless steel, for keeping oil at the right temperature (page 30).

Special items are the canned sea-urchin meat (page 171) (for using on spaghetti), the biscuits from Sardinia and the traditionally made panettone, with mini-sizes available as well (page 305).

Da Rosa

62 rue de Seine, 75006 Paris
Tel: 01 40 51 00 09

In his very beautiful food store/restaurant, Mr Da Rosa offers a range of excellent Mediterranean products.

Not to be missed: the salami products ... the exquisite Zibello culatello ham (page 96) and the lardo di Colonnata, aged for 18 months with 25 spices (page 101), the risotto rices and the black Venere rice (pages 205 and 211), the taggiasca olives, the Sicilian sauces, the preserves and the flavoured honeys imported by Apogei.

Bottega Pasta Vino

18 rue de Buci, 75006 Paris
Tel: 01 44 07 09 56

People go there for the legendary Signora (Madame) Inès, a real mamma, who gives you advice in her native tongue, with a Bolognese accent. At midday, her window overflows with good sandwiches (page 61). She also offers good 'home-made' meals: different sorts of lasagne (page 131), Roman-style gnocchi (page 199), fresh pasta and a large selection of traditionally made pasta.

La Grande Epicerie at Bon Marché

38 rue de Sèvres, 75007 Paris
Tel: 01 44 39 81 00
www.lagrandeepicerie.fr

Their shelves carry a very good representation of good Italian products. You will find, sold loose, pitted taggiasca olives (page 8), salted capers, pine nuts from Pisa, dried oregano branches, jars of Peck-brand mostarda (page 43), a good selection of panettone and pandoro at Christmas time or Colomba at Easter ... biscuits for making cakes (Saronno amaretti, Pavesini biscuits, amarena cherries).

In the Italian salami section, the Parma and San Daniele prosciutto sold by the slice have a little too much of their fat removed ... but are good quality. Try also the Neapolitan sausage (page 105) and the finocchiona (fennel sausage).

Idea Vino

88 avenue Parmentier 75010 Paris
Tel: 01 43 57 10 34

Carlo Dossi has created this temple of Italian wine: all the restaurateurs and individuals come to him to buy the best selection of wines from the Boot. Take advantage of Rita's recommendations to choose a good bottle from the 500 listings on offer! You can also find a large selection of grappa (eau-de-vie), liqueurs, digestifs and a quality grocery section (all of the Rustichella d'Abruzzo pasta shapes).

Amorino

4, rue de Buci, 75006 Paris
Other addresses at www.amorino.fr

Finally an Italian who has dared to create gelato shops like in Italy! The secret of Paolo Benassi's good gelato is his choice of very good ingredients to make them ... (fresh milk and eggs!) (pages 341 and 343).

These gelati are eaten as in Italy, not mixing too many different flavours together. Enjoying one pure flavour will always be preferred to American-style combinations.

You will find original flavours and the incredible focaccina, an orange-flower brioche filled with gelato. The version with Nutella-flavoured gelato is inimitable ... Soon, as in Italy, they will have soy or rice-milk-based gelato, for people with dairy intolerances.

acknowledgements

Grazie Mille!

To Pauline Ricard-André, stylist-decorator, for her efforts, advice and precious support.
To Grégoire Kalt, photographer, for his talent and enthusiasm.
We made a great team!

To all the shopkeepers who helped in the production of this book: Simona Restivo, Philippe Rebuzzi, Anna and Gian Paolo Chierici, Massimo Rizzo, the Davoli family, Rita Pruner, Sebastiano La Ferla, La Signora Ines, Mr Da Rosa, Rita and Carlo Dossi, Paolo Benassi.

To Rosemarie Di Domenico from Marabout who enabled me to produce this book.
To Ariadne Elisseeff for her passionate suggestions and assistance.
To Chiara Montini for her precious assistance.
To Emmanuelle Rivierre for her advice.

To my whole family who introduced me to the taste for good things.

To Philippe and Eva for their understanding and patience, and to all the friends who share and feed my passion.

shopping and address book

Alessi: plateware pp. 10, 15, 42, 113, 115, 117, 119, 136, 146, 158–159, 161, 209, 215, 241, 243, 253, 267
cutlery: pp. 76, 119, 191, 207, 213, 215, 217, 227, 235, 241, 275, 287, 299, 329
Saucepans pp. 110, 217, Frying pan p. 235
Driade: plateware pp. 148, 166, 191, 227, 229, 231, 245, 247, 251, 265, 271, 304.
glassware pp. 307, 337, 339
cutlery pp. 229, 231, 245, 247, 251.
Missoni Home: fabric pp. 146, 148, 209, 215, 217, 227, 241, 243, 245, 247, 314, 325, 339
plates by Richard Ginori pp. 207, 213, 307
Kitchen Bazaar: mini saucepans p. 157, mixing bowls pp. 169, 335, measuring spoons p. 177, strainer p. 183, apron p. 233, tart dish p. 311
Guzzini (at Kitchen Bazaar): mixing bowl and cutlery p. 180
Guzzini: mixing bowls pp. 233, 323, tart dish p. 329.
Rosenthal: cutlery pp. 183, 195, 243 plate p. 243, soup bowl p. 299, bowl p. 319
Virebent: plateware pp. 163, 281, 287, 313, 325
Frette: place mats pp. 166, 233, tablecloths pp. 313, 265
Ikea: apron p. 161
Habitat: apron pp. 190–191
Typhoon: oil bottle p. 297
Asa: tart dish p. 330.
Guy Degrenne: plate and fork p. 121
Missoni Home (textiles)

Lelièvre – show room
13 rue du Mail 75002 Paris/Tel: 01 43 16 88 00
Frette (textiles)
49 rue du Fg St Honoré 75008/Tel: 01 42 66 47 70
Missoni Home by Richard Ginori (plateware)
1 rue du faubourg St-Honoré, 75008 Paris
Tel: 01 44 51 96 96
Driade www.driade.com / mail: communications@driade.com
Dadriade via Manzoni 30 20121 Milano +39 02 76 00 59 59
Alessi
31 rue Boissy d'Anglas 75008 Paris/Tel: 01 42 66 31 00
Rosenthal Retail information: 01 53 34 04 44
Virebent Tel: 0148064417/
email: porcelaine.virebent.france@wanadoo.fr
Guy Degrenne www.Guydegrenne.com
Kitchen Bazaar
23 Bd de la Madeleine 75008 Paris/Tel: 01 42 60 50 30
Guzzini: Customer information line: 0810 13 73 72 and at Kitchen Bazar
www.habitat.net
www.ikea.fr
www. Asa-selection.de
www.typhooneurope.com

Published in 2009 by Murdoch Books Pty Limited
First published by Marabout (Hachette Livre) in 2006

Murdoch Books Australia
Pier 8/9
23 Hickson Road
Millers Point NSW 2000
Phone: +61 (0) 2 8220 2000
Fax: +61 (0) 2 8220 2558
www.murdochbooks.com.au

Murdoch Books UK Limited
Erico House, 6th Floor
93–99 Upper Richmond Road
Putney, London SW15 2TG
Phone: +44 (0) 20 8785 5995
Fax: +44 (0) 20 8785 5985
www.murdochbooks.co.uk

Publisher: Kay Scarlett

Project Editor: Livia Caiazzo
Design Concept: Marabout

Text copyright © Marabout 2006
The moral right of the author has been asserted.
Design copyright © Murdoch Books Pty Limited 2009

National Library of Australia Cataloguing-in-Publication Data

Author: Zavan, Laura.
Title: Little Italy / Laura Zavan.
ISBN: 9781741964356 (pbk.)
Notes: Includes index.
Subjects: Cookery, Italian.
                   Italy–Description and travel.
Dewey Number: 641.5945

A catalogue record for this book is available from the British Library.

Printed by 1010 Printing Interntional Limited in 2009. Printed in China.

IMPORTANT: Those who might be at risk from the effects of salmonella poisoning (the elderly, pregnant women, young children and those suffering from immune deficiency diseases) should consult their doctor with any concerns about eating raw eggs.

OVEN GUIDE: You may find cooking times vary depending on the oven you are using. For fan-forced ovens, as a general rule, set the oven temperature to 20°C (35°F) lower than indicated in the recipe.